SCOTNOTES
Number 46

The Gaelic Writings of Dòmhnall Mac na Ceàrdaich (Donald Sinclair)

Aonghas MacLeòid

Association for Scottish Literature 2025

Published by
Association for Scottish Literature
Scottish Literature
7 University Gardens
University of Glasgow
Glasgow G12 8QH

www.asls.org.uk

ASL is a registered charity no. SC006535

First published 2025

Text © Aonghas MacLeòid

All rights reserved. No part of this book may be reproduced, stored in a retrieval system, or transmitted in any form or means, electronic, mechanical, photocopying, recording or otherwise, without the prior permission of the Association for Scottish Literature.

A CIP catalogue for this title
is available from the British Library

ISBN 978-1-906841-64-5

Our authorised representative in the EU for product safety is JGU Scotland HUB, Johannes Gutenberg Universität Mainz
Jakob-Welder-Weg 18, 55128 Mainz, Germany
scotland@uni-mainz.de

ASL acknowledges the support of the
Scottish Government towards the publication of this book

CONTENTS

1	Dòmhnall Mac na Ceàrdaich (Donald Sinclair, 1885–1932)	1
2	His Literary Role	5
3	Drama: Gaelic History Maker	11
	Fearann a Shinnsir (*The Land of his Forebears*)	
	Crois-Tàra! (*The Call to Arms*)	
4	Short Stories	28
	Canach an t-Sléibhe (*The Muir Cotton*)	
	Uamh an Oir (*The Cave of Gold*)	
	Lughain Lir (*The Powers of the Sea*)	
5	Inbhe ar Bàrdachd (*The Development of Our Poetry*)	48
6	Poetry	55
	Faoileag an Droch-Chladaich (*The Gull of the Poor Shore*)	
	Òran air Deifir Beachd (*A Song on a Difference of Opinion*)	
	Loch na h-Ob	
	Fàilte do Bharraidh (*Welcome to Barra*)	
	A' Bheannachd Bharrach (*The Barra Blessing*)	
	Ròs Aluinn (*A Beautiful Rose*)	
	An Duradan Duslaich (*The Speck of Dust*)	
	Gairm Dùsgaidh (*Wake-Up Call*)	
	Slighe nan Seann Seun (*The Way of the Old Charms*)	
	Òran do na Fasain (*A Song to the Fashions*)	
	Cailleachan an t-Snaoisean (*The Old Women of Snuff*)	

CONTENTS (continued)

7	Là nan Seachd Sion (*The Day of the Seven Elements*)	80
8	Conclusion	90
9	Select Bibliography	92
10	Appendix: texts and translations of six poems of Dòmhnall Mac na Ceàrdaich	95

    Faoileag an Droch-Chladaich (*The Gull of the Poor Shore*) (1913)
    Cainnt mo Mhàthar (*My Mother Tongue*) (1914)
    Loch na h-Ob (1915)
    Ròs Aluinn (*A Beautiful Rose*) (1917)
    An Duradan Duslaich (*The Speck of Dust*) (1917)
    Slighe nan Seann Seun (*The Way of the Old Charms*) (1930)

THE ASSOCIATION FOR SCOTTISH LITERATURE aims to promote the study, teaching and writing of Scottish literature, and to further the study of the languages of Scotland.

To these ends, the ASL publishes works of Scottish literature; literary criticism and in-depth reviews of Scottish books in *Scottish Literary Review*; and scholarly studies of language in *Scottish Language*. It also publishes *New Writing Scotland*, an annual anthology of new poetry, drama and short fiction, in Scots, English and Gaelic. All these publications are available as a single 'package', in return for an annual subscription.

ASL also produces a range of teaching materials covering Scottish language and literature for use in schools.

Enquiries should be sent to:

    ASL
    Scottish Literature
    7 University Gardens
    University of Glasgow
    Glasgow G12 8QH

    Tel/fax +44 **(0)141 330 5309**
    e-mail **office@asls.org.uk**
    or visit our website at **www.asls.org.uk**

SCOTNOTES

Study guides to major Scottish writers and literary texts

Produced by the Education Committee
of the Association for Scottish Literature

Series Editors
Lorna Borrowman Smith
Dr Ronald Renton

Editorial Board
Dr Ronald Renton
(Convener, Education Committee, ASL)
Laurence Cavanagh
Professor John Corbett
Dr Emma Dymock
Dr Maureen Farrell
Dr Morna Fleming
Dr Simon Hall
John Hodgart
Bob Hume
Ann MacKinnon
Dr Maria Marchidanu
Professor Alan Riach
Dr Gillian Sargent
Dr Cheryl Simpson
Lorna Borrowman Smith
Andrew Young

A note on page references

Unless otherwise stated, all page references in this Scotnote are to the book *D.M.N.C.: Sgriobhaidhean Dhòmhnaill Mhic na Ceàrdaich* (*The Writings of Donald Sinclair*), edited by Lisa Storey (Clàr, 2014).

Acknowledgements

I'd like to thank Ronnie Renton for his assistance and encouragement in the production of this Scotnote, alongside Duncan Jones and Lorna Smith. John and Lisa Storey have been constant sources of encouragement in my work on Dòmhnall Mac na Ceàrdaich. This Scotnote would not have been possible without my M.Phil. thesis at the University of Glasgow, funded by a MacLean Teaching Assistantship and supervised by Dr Michel Byrne. Finally, I'm grateful to all those from Barra, Vatersay and Uist who have shown an interest or helped me with drawing attention to Mac na Ceàrdaich's literary achievements. Mòran taing dhuibh uile.

1. DÒMHNALL MAC NA CEÀRDAICH (DONALD SINCLAIR) 1885–1932

Dòmhnall Mac na Ceàrdaich is a crucial writer for those wishing to cast light upon the understudied crossroads of Gaelic literature in the early twentieth century. His work across poetry, drama, and prose examines and reflects a range of issues and concerns impacting on Gaelic literature. Prominent among these were Scottish Nationalism, the Celtic Revival and a self-confident Catholic identity that was establishing itself as a minority theme in the literature at the time. Whilst his work also reflects on more common themes in Gaelic literature of the time, such as land reform and migration, his enthusiastic use of multiple styles and categories of writing led to difficulties in how best to assess his contribution to that literature. However, as his work has been made accessible to a wider audience again his contribution to twentieth-century Gaelic literature is increasingly recognised. The full range of Mac na Ceàrdaich's work is beyond the scope of a short introductory volume but it is hoped that the present work will be useful to a range of audiences looking to engage with his writing, perhaps for the first time.

Mac na Ceàrdaich was born in Barra at the end of 1885 into an island that reflected the mix of prosperity and abject poverty found elsewhere in Victorian Scotland. The detailed testimony gathered by the Napier Commission in Barra two years previously paints a vivid portrait of a community stratified into those connected with the landowner on the one hand and crofters, fishermen and landless cottars on the other. Whilst the island had a developing herring fishery around the port of Castlebay, for those who were not involved in the trade and lacked access to agricultural land their existence was dire. This was exacerbated by the large areas of arable land that were under sheep farms, in which a few shepherds had replaced entire communities. This included the island of Vatersay, which Mac na Ceàrdaich's grandfather had once worked. The worst clearances on Barra had taken place thirty years previously and were still part of the living memory of much of the population.

In addition to the absolute poverty and the ongoing land struggles of the 1880s, Mac na Ceàrdaich was also directly impacted by the Education (Scotland) Act 1872. This act provided for education for every child, but did not make any provision for the Gaelic language. Mac na Ceàrdaich's academic aptitude and his family's prioritisation of education would lead to both him and his younger brother being engaged as student teachers at fourteen. Finding this unsuitable, Dòmhnall chose to go to sea with his father and older brothers. A teacher of Mac na Ceàrdaich's later recalled him composing songs at an early age and his time working at the herring fishing led to some of his earliest extant works.

Formal education provided by the Education Act was complemented by the oral tradition which continued in social gatherings in domestic settings – *taighean-cèilidh*. The contrast between the formal education that led to his material advancement and the deep-rooted cultural education he received in his home community would later be reflected in his work's scrutiny of different forms of knowledge and exploration of these cultural contrasts.

An opportunity for a more secure financial future opened up for Mac na Ceàrdaich in Scotland's industrial Central Belt. A Barra-born employee of Bruce Peebles in Edinburgh assisted with Mac na Ceàrdaich's hiring as an apprentice draughtsman at the electrical engineering firm, following their expansion into a new site at Pilton in 1904. At the time the company was manufacturing world-leading electrical engineering equipment, which was in demand in Scotland and elsewhere to power mine workings, tram systems and other heavy industries and utilities. Moving to Leslie Place, Stockbridge, Mac na Ceàrdaich would stay with fellow Barrach Calum Johnston and engaged with the literary world of Celtic Revivalists in the city including Alexander and Ella Carmichael, Skye bàrd Neil MacLeod and Professor Donald Mackinnon, inaugural Chair of Celtic at Edinburgh. The Revival was a multimedia phenomenon that influenced visual arts and architecture as well as literature and music across the Celtic nations of Europe. Particularly in Ireland, it was associated with a cultural self-confidence embodied by poets and dramatists such as W. B. Yeats, that would take a political direction with the armed Rising of 1916 and the eventual execution of cultural figures such as Pádraig Mac Piarais (*Patrick Pearse*), Thomas MacDonagh and Joseph Plunkett. In Edinburgh, figures such as Patrick Geddes had led a resurgence in the interest in Celtic art in different media. This included the visual arts with painters such as John Duncan as well as English-language writers such as William Sharp who used Celtic mythology and imagery as artistic inspiration.

Mac na Ceàrdaich, and his cousin Johnston, would have been familiar both with the Celtic Revival texts being published in Edinburgh and the source material of works like *Carmina Gadelica*, which featured folklore collected from Barra and elsewhere. Unlike Sorley MacLean a generation later, there is no sense that Mac na Ceàrdaich found the contrast between the polished published versions of such texts and the oral originals a matter for condemnation and he frequently used revival imagery in his work.

His status as an economic migrant, if not across international borders but certainly across cultural and then national boundaries, featured in his early work and remained an important theme throughout. Prior to the outbreak of the First World War, Mac na Ceàrdaich moved to Wembley where he remained until after the war working for British Westinghouse and then Metropolitan-Vickers, as the companies were variously amalgamated, acquired or reorganised. The barefooted boy from Castlebay was now working with world-leading technology in one of the most developed industrial cities on the planet.

Mac na Ceàrdaich's engineering work had another significant consequence for his artistic output. It most likely kept him in a protected occupation following the introduction of conscription during the First World War and, therefore, he did not serve at sea like many of his Barra contemporaries. Whether his pacifist views would have seen him sent to work with the conscientious objectors in the quarries of the North East of Scotland is not something that was ever put to the test. However, he did write an explicitly anti-war article towards the end of the war and pacifist themes are evident in his creative work from that time. In any case, the war years, when Mac na Ceàrdaich was working in England as an unmarried young man, were some of his most productive as regards his literary publications.

Mac na Ceàrdaich's work for Metropolitan-Vickers took him to Manchester. He was socially active amongst the Scottish industrial workers there and is listed as a convener of the local branch of the Scots National League in 1926, one of a series of political organisations founded or backed by Ruaraidh Erskine of Marr to advocate Scottish Home Rule. This would later be combined with the Glasgow University Scottish Nationalist Association in 1928 to form the National Party of Scotland, which following a further merger with the Scottish Party became the Scottish National Party in 1934. He also gave at least one lecture at the Manchester Celtic Society. His health would eventually decline, however, having contracted tuberculosis. He died in a sanitorium in Little Hulton, near Salford, in 1932.

2. HIS LITERARY ROLE

Mac na Ceàrdaich's literary world reflects the repeated transitions between the crofting and industrial contexts with which he was familiar, but also shows the chronological transition from the Celtic Revival and a European symbolist mysticism to the beginnings of the Scottish Renaissance and political modernism. In order to more fully understand his work, an appreciation of the context in which his work was produced, as well as how the poet thought of his own various literary traditions, is important.

We have seen from the biographical note the fundamental contrast between the industrial city with its advanced engineering and electrical draughtsmanship on the one hand, and the cottar fisherman life he was born into. Both societies had their problems with the smog of the city matched by the poverty of the cottars in Glen and Leideag on Barra. But for Mac na Ceàrdaich the economic opportunity of migration to the city was constantly being reassessed and contrasted with the pastoral beauties at home. This transition was repeated annually as he returned to Barra each summer before returning to life in Edinburgh, London and Salford thereafter. In Barra, he would collect proverbs and stay with his brother Neil, who was a school teacher and a later acquaintance of Compton Mackenzie, Fionn MacColla and Hugh MacDiarmid.

He was not just negotiating these two contrasting realisations of the prevailing economic order but he was by nature encyclopaedic in his interests in form and genre, covering nearly all of the various streams of printed Gaelic literature that were in print at the time. These ranged from the pedagogical endeavours of Presbyterian ministers such as Tormod MacLeòid (*Norman MacLeod*) in the mid-nineteenth century; anti-clearance invective of Uilleam MacDhun-Lèibhe (*William

Livingston); traditional-style songs and early Gaelic music-hall dramas. Mac na Ceàrdaich would also innovate with essays on poetics and nation-building; prose poems; symbolist mysticism and modern lyric poetry. This range places him simultaneously in the European mainstream as a committed writer engaging with his international context, as well as being an embodiment of a specific Gaelic legacy. The cosmopolitan aspect of his work is most obvious in his translations from Spanish, and his poems based on Persian originals. It is, however, an important, if not always obvious, feature throughout his writing.

The contrasting cultural situations in which he operated were not just a thematic tension in his creative work. Mac na Ceàrdaich's frustrations about infantilisation of the Gaels leads to him occasionally 'writing back' and may have informed his desire to innovate and utilise genres not readily associated with Gaelic literature in the nineteenth century. Whereas the English educationalist and Oxford professor Matthew Arnold, whose thinking influenced both the 1872 Education Act and the study of Celtic Literature, had declared that the Celts lacked the *architectonicé* for epic poetry and drama, Mac na Ceàrdaich the engineer, dramatist and epic poet dismisses these lines of thinking:

> Agus tuigidh sinn nach robh an Gàidheal cho 'glas' no cho mì-dhòigheil an seòl agus an alt innleachdan 's is toigh le fheadhainn an diugh (iad féin nach deanadh, ma dh' fhaoidte, spàin-lite) a chur as an leth.
> (*DMNC*, p. 345)

> *And we understand that the Gael wasn't so 'poor and undeveloped' or so unskilled in the ways and means of intellect as some people today (who themselves perhaps couldn't make a spurtle) like to assert on their behalf.*

That is not to say that the innovative Mac na Ceàrdaich was not fully engaged with the Gaelic oral tradition. Mac na Ceàrdaich's flatmate Calum Johnston, along with his sister Annie, would later be prolific informants for the School of Scottish Studies' folklore collections. It is difficult to comprehend, in fact, the level of literary knowledge possessed by people who were brought up in the oral tradition in Barra and Uist in 1900. Aside from the renowned *Carmina Gadelica*, which was one of the key texts in the Scottish Celtic Revival, informants like Nan Eachainn Fhionnlaigh (*Nan Mackinnon*), Seumas Iain Ghunnaraigh (*James MacKinnon*), Donnchadh mac Dhòmhnaill 'ic Dhonnchaidh (*Duncan MacDonald*) and scores more besides, would each be recorded and transcribed. Scholars such as Alexander Carmichael and later John Lorne Campbell and Calum Maclean variously attempted to describe the level of community knowledge that would feature at a taigh-cèilidh: a repertoire of thousands of songs and poems would be intermingled with hundreds of epic tales that could be told over several nights. Some of these tales were recorded in Irish and Scottish manuscripts centuries earlier, with Scotland maintaining some of the tales that had long since ceased to be found in Ireland.

This oral tradition of song and poetry also provided space for a creative impetus, which normalised and recognised poetic composition in the community alongside the ongoing transmission of traditional poetry and tales. Mac na Ceàrdaich continued to write songs for the community whilst working on his plays, lyrics and prose works. In continuing to write songs throughout much of his career Mac na Ceàrdaich stands athwart the classifications of bard-baile (*village poet*) versus nua-bhard (*modern poet*) that would later be used to categorise mid-twentieth-century poets. It is not just in his person as a innovative lyric poet who continued to write community songs that this division breaks down. The works themselves highlight the problem with the dichotomy, as some of his songs use formal, high-register language and a range of modern poetic techniques, rather than renegotiate existing motifs and stock images for ready transmission and retention.

In thinking about Mac na Ceàrdaich and how he relates to other published Gaelic poets there are a number of key influences who should be born in mind. One of these is Alasdair Mac Mhaighstir Alasdair *(Alexander MacDonald,* c. 1691–1760). Mac na Ceàrdaich and he shared a political understanding of poetry, a desire to demonstrate Gaelic's abilities as a modern language suitable for contemporary literature; a view of Gaelic in a broader Scottish and Celtic context and a West Coast Catholic culture. As a writer Mac Mhaighstir Alasdair was responsible for the first collection of secular Gaelic verse with his *Ais-Eiridh na Sean Chánoin Albannach* (*The Resurrection of the Ancient Scottish Tongue*) appearing in print in 1751. His use of the long poem, particularly his sea epic 'Beannachadh Luinge' or 'Birlinn Chlann Raghnaill' (*'Ship's Blessing'* or *'Clanranald's Birlinn'*), is the most apparent influence on Mac na Ceàrdaich, but the outward-looking yet intensely political approach to literature is there at a more fundamental level.

The publication of Mac na Ceàrdaich's work is inseparable from the influence of Ruaraidh Erskine of Marr. As his title suggests he was minor gentry, who had learned Gaelic from his Hebridean nanny. He was dedicated to Home Rule, having been involved with the Scottish Home Rule Association in the 1890s, and his journal *Guth na Bliadhna* (*The Voice of the Year*) provided a home to radical nationalist Gaelic writing. This journal ran fairly regularly from the 1890s into the 1920s and its most regular period of appearance coincides with Mac na Ceàrdaich's most prolific period of publication. It was also an important outlet of Catholic Gaelic thinking, featuring articles by clergymen as well as by Irish cultural nationalists such as Douglas Hyde. Prior to the arrival of Ruaraidh MacThòmais (*Derick Thomson*) in the 1950s, Erskine of Marr was the editor who did the most to promote innovative Gaelic writing. Erskine would also go on to found and fund *The Scots Independent* in 1926, which published Mac na Ceàrdaich's creative pieces and columns as the first Gaelic columnist of this still extant nationalist newspaper.

Erskine of Marr is the likely avenue through which Mac na Ceàrdaich became acquainted with Christopher Murray Grieve, who as Hugh MacDiarmid edited a number of Mac na Ceàrdaich's pieces in the Erskine-funded *Pictish Review*. Perhaps more so than any other contemporary writer, including Mac na Ceàrdaich's fellow Gaels, MacDiarmid promoted Mac na Ceàrdaich's writing both at the time and posthumously by including the lyric 'Slighe nan Seann Seun' ('*The Way of the Old Spells*') in his canon-building *A Golden Treasury of Scottish Poetry*. This ensured that at least one of Mac na Ceàrdaich's poems could be described as 'much anthologised' in collections focusing on the early and mid-twentieth century. MacDiarmid was clearly moved by his friend's early death and wrote a eulogy that compares him to other significant poets of his day including W. B. Yeats and T. S. Eliot and draws parallels with Mac Mhaighstir Alasdair's role in the literature.

The importance of contemporary Catholic theology to 'Là nan Seachd Sìon' ('*The Day of the Seven Elements*'), as well as Mac na Ceàrdaich's other works, was in and of itself innovative. Despite having remained a sizeable minority of the Gaelic-speaking population since the Reformation, the Catholic community's contribution to Scottish Gaelic literature had been relegated by some scholars to a preserver of folk traditions, lost elsewhere due to the zeal of nineteenth-century evangelicalism. Both aspects of this view are now being questioned. Father Allan McDonald, born in Fort Willliam but based for many years in Eriskay and South Uist, was a productive poet, as well as lexicographer and folklore collector who died aged forty-six in 1905. Mac na Ceàrdaich was familiar with his work, as he published a long traditional prayer that was found in Fr Allan's papers. This self-confident Gaelic Catholic culture, abetted by Erskine of Marr, was one of a variety of contributory factors that led to Gaelic literature in the early years of the twentieth century being more diverse and vibrant than has been recognised.

Mac na Ceàrdaich was occasionally published in outlets other than the radical publications of Erskine of Marr, notably *The Celtic Review* edited by Ella Carmichael. Given his productive output it is noticeable that he only appears once in an An Comunn Gàidhealach publication: the 1927 *Voices from the Hills* anthology. As the largest Gaelic cultural organisation of the time they published significant amounts of writing during the period. The pattern of ignoring his work by anthologists continued, with Mac na Ceàrdaich being passed over for An Comunn Gàidhealach's school anthologies including those edited by Seumas MacThòmais (*James Thomson*). MacThòmais had appeared in the same periodicals as Mac na Ceàrdaich and would likely have been familiar with his work.

Mac na Ceàrdaich's role has been noted by later anthologists especially Ronald Black in his comprehensive survey *An Tuil: An Anthology of 20th Century Scottish Gaelic Verse*, but it was not until Mac na Ceàrdaich's relation, publisher Lisa Storey, edited a comprehensive edition of his writings in 2014 that his work became accessible to contemporary readers once again. Entitled *D.M.N.C.*, following the writer's use of his Gaelic initials alone to identify him as the author for most of his published works, Storey's edition demonstrated the diversity and extent of Mac na Ceàrdaich's writings. It also included many songs published for the first time, taken from manuscript.

3. DRAMA: GAELIC HISTORY MAKER

Mac na Ceàrdaich's six plays fall into three distinct genres. His first two could be termed community dramas: comedies that rely on well-known characters and plot devices to entertain the audience whilst touching on more serious issues. The second two plays are historical dramas focusing on transformative events in Highland history. His final two plays are children's plays featuring motifs from the Gaelic mythology common to Scotland and Ireland. His historical plays are most noteworthy as some of the earliest examples of committed theatre for a Gaelic audience, as opposed to the more community or theatre hall entertainment of the earliest plays. As well as re-enacting historical debates, they present pressing questions of contemporary relevance to the audience.

Published in *Guth na Bliadhna* in 1913, *Fearann a Shinnsir* (*The Land of his Forebears*) is based on the clearances from Barra in the mid-nineteenth century, with a substantial timespan and geographical spread taking characters from the Hebrides to Canada and back. *Crois-Tàra!* (*The Call to Arms!*), which followed in 1914, is set during the 1745–46 Jacobite Rising. It commences as Charles Edward Stuart arrives on the Scottish mainland, and concludes after he departs for France from the West Highlands. Both plays focus on moments of crisis for the Gaelic-speaking community, and share a similar genesis in that they were published either side of the outbreak the First World War when the world was entering a period of grave crisis and the Highlands had been witnessing frequent land raids on the estates of the gentry.

Fearann a Shinnsir (1913) (*The Land of his Forebears*)
Fearann a Shinnsir (*DMNC*, pp. 199–227) was Mac na Ceàrdaich's first published historical play. The play looks at

a family who are evicted during the Highland Clearances and forced to emigrate to Canada before returning to their native island. As a piece of theatre it processes both historic trauma and dramatises contemporary political debates, whilst also telling an accessible tale of love and redemption.

The play commences in a Barra-esque Hebridean setting with Dòmhnull Pìobaire, his wife Caitrìona and son Alasdair undertaking everyday crofting tasks. A dream Caitrìona mentions serves as a premonition of the trauma to come, which is confirmed by the arrival of the Maor (*Factor* or *Bailiff*) who serves an eviction notice whilst Alasdair is absent. The second act looks at the eviction itself, with Mac na Ceàrdaich focusing on the Fear a' Bhaile (*Tacksman/Tenant Farmer*) and Maor physically driving the elderly couple to the quayside, despite Alasdair's vigorous protestations. The third act has Alasdair emerge as the clear protagonist whose parents have subsequently died in Canada. His lover, who appears briefly in disguise in Act II to bid farewell, summons him back to Scotland urgently. Alasdair duly returns in Act IV, preventing her marriage to the increasingly sexually aggressive Factor in whose house she works as a domestic servant. The Tacksman, we find out, is repenting his previous conduct. Despite Alasdair listing the extent of the Tacksman's misdemeanours, Alasdair is convinced to forgive him his treatment of Dòmhnull and Caitrìona by Mòrag's appeals to Alasdair's religious convictions and the comprehensive nature of Fear a' Bhaile's contrition.

This redemption of one of the two main antagonists, who is forgiven by the protagonist at the play's conclusion, as well as the rather formulaic love story, have led to the play being called 'rather naïve'. However focusing on the formulaic, or indeed accessible, elements of the plot seems to miss the point of a communal exploration of the issues facing the islanders on Barra in 1851 and 1913. It is equally true that, whilst Mac na Ceàrdaich was an ardent land reformer, he was not a class-war Marxist, and the restitution of the land to the protagonist, Alasdair, accompanied by honest contrition leads to the restoration of relations between the tenant and tacksman classes.

The protagonist Alasdair Dhòmhnuill Phìobaire is the most sophisticatedly developed of Mac na Ceàrdaich's dramatic characters. In part, the lengthy chronology of the play allows this to occur as the play moves from the deception and outrage of the clearances to the eventual restoration of the land and reconciliation. His initial indignation and oath-taking that follows the injustice of his parents being served notice foreshadows the conclusion with Alasdair swearing at the end of Act I:

> Mur is mise mac m' athar agus mo mhàthar, mo bheatha agus mo shaoghal gu'n naisg mi as leth an còraichean gus am faigh ceartas buaidh agus ana-cheartas a dhuais!
> (*DMNC*, p. 203)

> *If I'm not my father and mother's son, my life and my world I will bind to their rights until justice prevails and injustice receives its deserts!*

Alasdair is immediately cautioned by his father for making 'bòidean baoth' ('*vain oaths*'), and the fatalistic attitudes of Dòmhnull and Caitrìona contrast with Alasdair's sense of injustice in Acts I and II. Both parents have a certainty in divine justice which Alasdair does not, with Dòmhnull stating:

> Cho cinnteach 's a tha nèamh agus talamh gheibh an eucoir a duais dhligheach a bhos no thall. [...] Feumaidh tu misneach agus treun-earbsa a chur anns an Fhreasdal gu'n gléidh E thu bho bheud.
> (*DMNC*, pp. 203–04)

As surely as there is a heaven and earth, crime will get its just rewards here or hereafter. [...] You need to put confidence and certain trust in Providence, that He will save you from harm.

In Act III, Alasdair is despondent about the situation in Canada where he is living alone following the death of his parents. However, the arrival of firstly another Gaelic speaker, then his brother, and finally a letter from Caitrìona restore both a hope and sense of personal agency to him, providing the motivation to return to the Hebrides for the finale.

Alasdair's dialogue and sense of injustice are the vehicles by which Mac na Ceàrdaich best indicts the conduct and ideas of the landlords. Act II is used to highlight some of the arguments against the landed gentry that were a feature of progressive politics in Scotland in 1913. These appear in an increasingly hot-tempered exchange between him and Fear a' Bhaile (*The Tacksman*). Alasdair initially asks what gives him the authority to destroy a community:

Co a thug dhuit-sa còir air beatha an t-sluaigh no air tiodhlaicean a chaidh fhàgail aca? An tusa, a tha 'n diugh, ar leat féin, uile-chumhachdach ad ghniomh 's ad fhacal: an tusa, tha mi faighneachd, a tha gabhail de dhànadas agus de ladarnas gu'n canadh tu: 'Le m' fhacal-sa théid na ceudan a sgiursadh bho thìr an dùthchais.'
(*DMNC*, p. 206)

Who gave you the right over the lives of the people and the inheritances that were left to them? Is it you, who are today, in your eyes, omnipotent in your deeds and words: is it you, I'm asking, who are so bold and arrogant to say: 'By my word hundreds will be persecuted from their homeland.'

When he is told that it is the authority vested in the landowner by virtue of being the landowner, Alasdair questions the manner in which he came to possess the land, and the competing claims of legal owner versus longstanding inhabitants of that land. This reflects the arguments collated by Tom Johnston in his influential *Our Scots Noble Families* (1909). This was a collection of articles that outlined the frequently nefarious manner in which the aristocracy had acquired, enclosed and retained land over the centuries, to make evident to readers that the wealth accrued had not been done by honest means. Indeed, in more recent years, we have seen that both the proceeds of, and latterly compensation related to, chattel slavery also helped fund the clearance schemes of the so-called 'improvers'.

Alasdair therefore contrasts this lazy entitlement of the Tacksman with the physical ties of the community to the land:

> ALASDAIR: 'S ann, leat-sa a tha 'm fearann. Smaointich, a dhuine gun iochd, air gu dé mar a fhuair thu e. Gu dé mar a fhuair do dhaoine e, agus co a cheannaich le am fuil e, agus a chuir an ìre e le falus an gruaidheach. [...] Canaidh tu gu'n d' fhuair thu e mar chòir-bhreith, no gu'n do choisinn thu e air dhòigheiginn: dìreach sin – ma fhuair 's e a fhuair thu, a dhuine, còir a bhi a' togail riadh na braid a chaidh a dheanamh mu'n do rugadh do shì-sheanair.
> (*DMNC*, pp. 206–07)

> ALASDAIR: *The land belongs to you. Think, man without mercy, of how you acquired it. How your people got it, and who bought it with their blood and developed it with the sweat of their brow. [...] You say that you got it as a birthright, or that you earned it somehow: exactly that – if you got it, what you got, man, was the right to take interest from the theft that was done before your great-grandfather was born.*

It's not just Alasdair who is used to voice wider political arguments. Whilst the Maor and Fear a' Bhaile are clearly the villains of the piece, Mac na Ceàrdaich uses them to create a contrast between the improvement rhetoric of Act I and the brutal reality of clearance in Act II. The Maor advises:

> 'S e bu chòir a bhi 'nar cridhe taingealachd agus buidheachas do dh' fhear-solair ur leas, agus cha 'n e a bhi a' cur an-diu air cobhair an àm 'ur feuma.
> (*DMNC*, p. 202)
>
> *We should have gratitude and gratefulness in our hearts for the provider of your improvement, and not be despising help in your hour of need.*

He attempts to reframe the situation as an invitation to take an opportunity, rather than being an eviction summons. The contrast with him harrying the elderly couple towards the quay in the following act, dramatises the contrast between the polite ideals of 'improvement' and the brutal realities of eviction.

We know from testimony collected by Donald MacLeod in his series of accounts of the clearances entitled *Gloomy Memories*, that the evictions in Barra in 1851 were particularly barbarous and closely resemble the scenes in Act II of the play. This included the use of dogs, as well as the whips and irons referred to by Mac na Ceàrdaich. Moreover, the play also reflects the forced evictions that followed on from the paternalistic portrayals of voluntary emigration that preceded them. The historical parallels extend to the misery in Canada in Act III, with the dire state of the Barra emigrants chronicled in the Canadian press at the time. This history was still being passed down orally in Barra whilst Mac na Ceàrdaich was writing. One version of the story of the evictions was published from the narration of Mac na Ceàrdaich's near-contemporary An Codaidh (*John MacPherson*) in *Tales From Barra*. The public reenactment of this collective trauma would have been an extraordinarily powerful moment of theatre in Castlebay, and other communities impacted by clearance, whilst making the politics of land reform accessible to a wider audience.

We also know from *Gloomy Memories* that the Maor's designs on Mòrag reflect not just a trope that was common in plays with aristocratic villains, but also the brutal reality of life in the Hebrides under the landlord system. The co-signed testimony witnessed by poet Uilleam MacDhunlèibhe (*William Livingston*) and Gaelic publisher Archibald Sinclair in 1852 is frank in this regard. The recently evicted Barra crofters thought that D. W. McGillvray [*sic*], the local Tacksman and Justice of the Peace who had tried to discredit their published accounts with *ad hominen* attacks 'should be last to speak of "illegitimate children", as a poor idiotic female [...] fathered a child on him, and declared that various stratagems were tried to prevent disclosures' (*Gloomy Memories*, pp. 137–38).

Aside from the relevance of the 1851 clearances to the play, Mac na Ceàrdaich's contemporary radical context is important for understanding *Fearann a Shinnsir*'s production, reception and significance. Land raiding was a feature of Gaelic politics emerging regularly throughout the nineteenth and into the mid-twentieth century. In essence it involved the establishment of agricultural and/or domestic holdings by landless cottars on land owned by the usually absentee landlord, without that landlord's consent. Symbolically, it was also a public rejection of the claims of the propertied classes and laws of land ownership that governed the Highlands, often involving the arguments used by Alasdair in Act II.

This was a personal concern for Mac na Ceàrdaich, who watched in court as his cousins were imprisoned in Edinburgh in 1908 as a result of staking out crofts and building houses on the island of Vatersay. This fertile island sat directly across the bay from where many of Barra's impoverished cottars had been living since the clearances. He and several other poets memorialised the event in song, with Mac na Ceàrdaich saying:

> Tha m' aigneadh air cinntinn cho àrd
> 'S mo chridhe cho làn le sùrd
> Bho'n chunnaic mi cuideachd mo ghràidh
> A' suidhe Dimàirt aig cùirt.
> [...]
> Ged tha sibh an diugh far nach àill
> 'S nach fhaic sibh 'ur càird car ùin'
> Na cuireadh sin tuisleadh na'r càil
> Oir's tiugh tha na sàir ri'r cùl.
>
> (*DMNC*, pp. 111–12)

My spirits have grown so high / And my heart so full of delight / Since I saw my beloved company / Sitting on Tuesday in court. / [...] / Although today you're where you'd not wish / And you will see no friends for a time / Don't let that blunt your vigour / As the heroes are lined deep at your back.

The regular rhyme-scheme and initial instruction for the poem to be sung to the tune of a well-known song make clear that this is a poem for community transmission and consumption. The proclaimed solidarity of the Gaels and the personal impact of the news of the events on the poet's spirits are most readily comparable with that of the Land League poets a generation earlier, notably Màiri Mhòr nan Òran (*Mary MacPherson*) and Dòmhnall MacCaluim (*Rev. Donald MacCallum*) who composed songs on the 1880s Crofters' War.

But influences from outside the Gàidhealtachd are also apparent in the play. Given the prominence of religious ideas throughout, *Fearann a Shinnsir* should also be considered in light of Catholic Social Teaching. This developed notably under Leo XIII, whose encyclical *Rerum Novarum* acknowledged the problems that were evident in capitalist society in the 1880s but rejected the various socialist and communist programmes for addressing these:

> The great mistake made in regard to the matter now under consideration is to take up with the notion that class is naturally hostile to class, and that the wealthy and the working men are intended by nature to live in mutual conflict. [...] Each needs the other: capital cannot do without labour, nor labour without capital. Mutual agreement results in the beauty of good order, while perpetual conflict necessarily produces confusion and savage barbarity. Now, in preventing such strife as this, and in uprooting it, the efficacy of Christian institutions is marvellous and manifold. First of all, there is no intermediary more powerful than religion (whereof the Church is the interpreter and guardian) in drawing the rich and the working class together, by reminding each of its duties to the other, and especially of the obligations of justice.

Whilst the reconciliation at the conclusion of the play between Alasdair and Fear a' Bhaile following the latter's contrition can strike readers as naïve, certainly from a class-based perspective, it does convey Mac na Ceàrdaich's views or at least posit a question as to what are the obligations towards forgiveness on a Catholic character:

> ALASDAIR: 'Math dhuinn ar fiachan mar mhathas sinne do luchd-ar-fiach!' [...] Sìth mata gu'n robh deanta, agus réite

gu'n robh eadarainn! Sìth gu'n robh agaibh a bhos agus thall oir fanaidh mise air sgàth Moraig, agus gabhaidh as ùr agus as nodha mo sheilbh air fearann mo shinnsir!
(*DMNC*, p. 227)

ALASDAIR: *'Forgive us our trespasses as we forgive those who trespass against us!' [...] Let peace be made and reconciliation be between us. May peace be with you here and afar, for I will stay because of Morag, and will take possession afresh and once more of the land of my forebears!*

Crois-Tàra!¹ (1914) (*The Call to Arms!*)

His second historical play *Crois-Tàra!* (*DMNC*, pp. 228–67) is set during the Jacobite rising of 1745–46, focusing on the decisions of the gentry and tenants who took part in it on behalf of the Stuart dynasty. As such, response to crisis is perhaps the central structuring principle of the play, which allows it to explore topics such as duty, honour, obligation, shame and poetic incitement to military action. The play also includes a romance but this seems rather perfunctory in comparison to the discussions on the duties of the major characters. Like many of Mac na Ceàrdaich's songs these plays are for popular consumption, albeit in a minoritised culture, and are crafted to reflect the expectations of the audience. The comedic ending, with the successful conclusion of the love affair of the hero, is a direct reflection of this, similar to some of the plot devices in *Fearann a Shinnsir*.

Mac na Ceàrdaich uses the Rising to examine the various

---

1   A more literal translation is The Fiery Cross. Edward Dwelly defines it in his dictionary as 'The gathering beam, a signal formerly used on occasions of insult or impending danger to summon a clan to arms. It was a piece of wood, half burnt and dipped in blood, in token of the revenge of fire and sword awaiting those clansmen who did not immediately answer the summons.'

reactions to the news of the Prince's arrival. This gives him scope to interrogate themes of pressing relevance to his contemporaries whilst critiquing some of the imperialist Scottish and Gaelic jingoism of the day. One of the means the writer uses to do this is by placing the major eighteenth-century poet Alasdair Mac Mhaighstir Alasdair amongst the characters of the play. There was a historical basis for doing this as Mac Mhaighstir had served as a captain in the Jacobite army and was present at the battles of Prestonpans and Culloden. After the Rising he published the first collection of Gaelic secular verse in the explicitly nationalist and Jacobite *Ais-Eiridh na Sean Chánoin Albannaich* (*Resurrection of the Old Scottish Language*). As outlined above he also stands as a father figure to poetry in Modern Scottish Gaelic literature, so Mac na Ceàrdaich's portrayal of him as a bombastic chauvinist is of immediate interest.

For all that Mac na Ceàrdaich admired the poet's work, one of the themes in *Crois-Tàra!* is to help explore poetic culpability in inciting military conflict and the responsibility for its subsequent impacts. Mac Mhaighstir Alasdair appears in the first scene in the Laird of Borrodale's reception room convinced of the military superiority of the Gaels and of the justness of their cause. This hubris, or pride that will lead to the undoing of most of the major characters in the play, is shared by Borrodale himself. Both characters quickly close down the voicing of any doubts as to the ultimate success of their cause. This is done initially by Mac Mhaighstir Alasdair who casts his doubts on both the loyalty and courage of Eoghan:

> An e do chreud-sa, a Mhic Dhùghaill air t' ainm, an eucoir agus an donas? An e gu'n do reic thusa t' anam agus do cholainn ri ceann-feadhna nan tràill agus nan trusdar?
> (*DMNC*, p. 229)

> *Is your creed, by your name Mac Dougall, crime and wickedness? Is it that you have sold your soul and your body to the chief of slaves and lechers?*

Eoghan's practical concerns about a lack of military support and capacity are deliberately and repeatedly recast in the scene as a moral failure on his part. Borrodale follows Mac Mhaighstir Alasdair's lead:

> 'S mi-fhearail, 'Eòghain Dhòmhnullaich, do spiorad agus is mi-chliùiteach am beus a bhith a' cur droch mhanaidh air ionnsuidh so na h-Albann as leth a righ agus saorsa!
> (*DMNC*, p. 230)

> *It is unmanly, Ewan MacDonald, in spirit and unworthy in morals to put such ill omens on this campaign of Scotland's on behalf of the King and of Freedom!*

The arrival of a chorus of clansmen further amplifies this crushing of dissent as they say in unison:

> Na abair e! 'Eoghain Mhic Dhùghaill, na maslaich e! Co e nach togadh a chlaidheamh as leth Thearlaich Stiubhart, Prionnsa nan Gàidheal!
> (*DMNC*, p. 230)

> *Don't say it! Ewan son of Dougal, do not disgrace it! Who wouldn't lift his sword on behalf of Charles Stuart, Prince of the Gaels!*

With its 1914 wartime context, Mac Mhaighstir Alasdair's character is a crucial one for considering what questions the play asks of the audience. With a level of self-scrutiny that is typical of Mac na Ceàrdaich, he scrutinises the role of poets and artists in encouraging ethnic chauvinism by creating and reinforcing ideals of duty, honour and shame. This sees practical and political questions being reframed as questions of loyalty, in order to limit dissent, as occurs in Act I. *Crois-Tàra!* makes clear the catastrophic consequences of this process.

This silencing of critical voices is supplemented by rhetorical bombast when the Chief of Clanranald asks Mac Mhaighstir Alasdair to give the official response from the clan to the Prince. Mac Mhaighstir Alasdair commences his address to the Prince in a courtly fashion before whipping himself up into a frenzy of over-the-top pledges of allegiance and apocalyptic imagery:

> Ged dh' éireadh feachdan an domhain 'nan aon tonn cumhachd 'nar n-aghaidh; ged dh' éireadh mairbh naimhdean mhìle bliadhna bho 'n leapannan-crionaidh; ged ghairmeadh an domhain rùn sgrios nan dùl g'ar slugadh suas. Seadh, – ged dh' fhosgladh Iutharna 'na mhìlte craos a leigeil as feachd a mhìltean deomhan 'nar n-aghaidh, cha ghéill, – cha tréig, – cha lasaich, – cha till, cha sguir sinn gus an dìoghail sinn làn an aicheamhail, gus an coilion sinn buileach an éirig! (*DMNC*, p. 237)

> *Though the forces of the world would rise up in one powerful wave against us; though the dead enemies of a thousand years rose from their ruined beds; though the world called a death wish of elements on us to swallow us. Yes, – even if hell opened its thousand gullets letting out hosts of thousands of demons against us, we will not yield, – we will not abandon, – we will not weaken, – we will not turn and we will not stop until we fully avenge the reprisals and we are entirely recompensed!*

This officially sanctioned, effusive response is in stark contrast to the debates that opened the play and to the notices from

Macdonald of Sleat and MacLeod of Harris, advising the Prince that they are not in a position to support him. These arrive shortly before Mac Mhaighstir Alasdair begins his incitement.

Mac na Ceàrdaich therefore uses the debate and dialogue to posit questions about loyalty, dissent, and cultural complicity in irrational wartime incitement. But he also uses the audience's awareness of the subsequent defeat of the Rising to explore the theme of fate. Similar to the Greek tragedies, where the outcome was also usually known in advance, Mac na Ceàrdaich is creating a compelling tragic framework for one of the first times in Scottish Gaelic theatre.

The role of fate in human affairs appears in the debate in Act I, with Mac Dougall, the patronymic of the sceptically inclined Eoghan Dòmhnullach, arguing against Borrodale and Mac Mhaighstir Alasdair at the opening:

> Dàn! 'S minig a dheilbh neach an don-gnothuich a dhàn féin agus is tric a chuir teas an teine faoin-chruadal an cridhe gun eòlas.
> (*DMNC*, p. 228)

> *Fate! Many a time has an ill-deed's author designed his own fate and often has the heat of the fire put an idiotic determination in a clueless heart.*

Mac Mhaighstear Alasdair's final words in Act IV of the play clearly echo this earlier debate, with him claiming: 'Ach bha e 'n dàn, bha e 'n dàn!' (*DMNC*, p. 265) ('*But it was destined, it was destined!*') This neatly absolves himself from any moral culpability in the failure of the Rising that he had vigorously incited in Act I, as well as absolving his fellow gentry of their decision-making's undoubted role in the suffering inflicted upon the ordinary tenants, as seen in Act III.

Related to this discussion on fate, the tragic structure also allows Mac na Ceàrdaich to examine the role of duty in the decisions of the main characters, in as much as they are not acting out of an estimation of the likelihood of success but rather on a moral basis of duty. These themes of duty and fate interact throughout the discussions about right conduct. The second act in particular looks at how one Clanranald tenant, Dòmhnull Mac Eachainn, who served in 1715 reacts to the news that Charles Edward Stuart intends to lead a second Rising. At its outset he is busy looking for his old sword in the chest where he had left it. He is only content not to join the rest of his clan when his chief advises him that he has fulfilled his 'dleasnas' (*'duty'*) and his enthusiastic son may come in his place.

Duty and virtue, and the role of shame in maintaining this system are particularly important given Gaelic poetry's traditions of praise poetry and satire. Mac na Ceàrdaich is again aware of the relationships between poetic skills and the interests of rulers looking to maintain the duty-based system of military service and other clan obligations. The Gaelic poetry of preceding centuries, in both vernacular and classical Gaelic, took for granted a system of praise that celebrated a chief as a generous, just leader and competent military commander, whether as a reflection of reality or to encourage better conduct. Bards who were maintained by clan chiefs in their local courts could shame the gentry into supporting their work financially or changing their behaviour. The same shared imagery, defined by scholar John MacInnes as a 'panygeric code', is found in the anonymous songs of women poets and in the waulking songs from the period. So whilst Mac na Ceàrdaich's original audience would not have been familiar with the later codification of this system, they would have understood the role of shame and praise directly, in the traditional Gaelic song corpus.

Mac na Ceàrdaich utilises the setting and four-act structure of the play to good effect. The first act commences in the Laird of Borrodale's reception room as the Clanranald gentry, and the audience, await the arrival of the prince. This builds tension and anticipation whilst the discussion on what is the right course of action takes place. It also places the start of the play at the start of the Rising on the mainland, and the final act focuses on the very end of the Rising as the Prince sails for France.

This national scope envelops the domestic setting of the middle two acts of the play, which are set in the household of the old tenant Dòmhnull Mac Eachainn. The arrival of the Prince and the aristocracy in this humbler setting contrasts the idealism of the gentry with the reality of what their decisions mean for the wider population. The impact of the Rising is most clearly illustrated in Act III when two Hanovarian soldiers raid the house in search of Jacobite fugitives. Without this domestic focus, the play would not provide the same scrutiny of the impact of the decisions of the aristocracy on the life of the wider population. In its 1914 wartime context, where suffrage and parliamentary representation was still heavily restricted by sex, age and class, it reinforces the impact of a reckless bravura amongst a society's leadership on the lives of everyone else.

As in *Fearann a Shinnsir*, Mac na Ceàrdaich uses a romance between two of the characters that seems a bit perfunctory. The old tenant Dòmhnull's son Raonull and Oighrig briefly express their regret as Raonull is preparing to depart in Act II, with Raonull emphasising the duty of the MacDonalds to support the prince. Oighrig then reappears at the play's conclusion to reunite with Raonull and Dòmhnull in a comedic or unifying ending, once the Prince has departed. However, it's the old Clanranald tenant Dòmhnull who has the last word: 'Tha mo spiorad a' gabhail a chead do dh' ìmpidh nan treun.

Tha m'anam ag iarraidh gu dachaidh nam Flathas far nach cluinn mi tuille "Crois-tàra!"' (*DMNC*, p. 267) ('*My spirit takes its leave of the exhortations of strongmen. My soul wants home to paradise, where I will hear "Crois-tàra!"* [*the call to arms*] *no more!*').

In the context of 1914, these questions of duty, and the role of poets in promoting ideals of military virtue and honour are brought sharply into focus. Whilst it was perhaps too early for even pacifistic poets to envision the scale of what the commencement of war would entail, Mac na Ceàrdaich's questioning of co-option by the British Empire of Gaelic ideals of honour was an important counter-narrative to the prevailing winds of service to the empire. The role that literature and the arts played in honouring the British Empire and militarism more generally, and in maintaining the hubris that contributed to war is contrasted with the suffering of the tenant family. *Crois-Tàra!* has an important place in pacifist literature in that, whilst Gaelic-speaking pacifists such as Alasdair MacNeacail (*Alexander Nicolson*), uncle of Sorley MacLean, were imprisoned alongside other conscientious objectors, their views have not been well represented in the written literature from the period. In both *Fearann a Shinnsir* and *Crois-Tàra!*, therefore, Mac na Ceàrdaich makes his views on politics known pointedly throughout, despite there being a happy ending of sorts in each play.

4. SHORT STORIES

Mac na Ceàrdaich's ambitions for Gaelic literature are as evident in his short stories as they are in his drama. Commencing with the Celtic Revival-style repurposing of old tales, such as the Deirdire tale in 1915's 'Canach an t-Sléibhe' (*'The Muir Cotton'*) (*DMNC*, pp. 377–83) or the piper and his hound disappearing into 'Uamh an Oir' (*'The Cave of Gold'*) (*DMNC*, pp. 391–98) from 1917, Mac na Ceàrdaich starts with themes and styles that are familiar to him and his audience. But he also experiments, as he did in other genres, with both structure and styles that were innovative for Gaelic writing, creating one of the first recognisably modern short stories in Gaelic with 1921's 'Lughain Lir' (*'The Powers of the Sea'*) (*DMNC*, pp. 399–421) and writing increasingly allegorical and poetic prose such as 1927's 'Dealachadh nan Rathad' (*'The Parting of the Ways'*) (*DMNC*, pp. 426–31).

Canach an t-Sléibhe (1915) (*The Muir Cotton*)
As a retelling of the popular folktale of Deirdire, *Canach an t-Sléibhe* (*DMNC*, pp. 377–83) is very much a reflection of the Celtic Revival movement, where writers such as Yeats and painters such as John Duncan revisited Gaelic folklore for inspiration. An oral version of the Deirdire story had been collected in Barra by Alexander Carmichael, and published with translation in 1905, illustrated in a Celtic Revival Style.

Mac na Ceàrdaich's short story looks at an early stage of the longer tale, when Deirdire is living in ignorance of the outside world and the bloody end that has been prophesied for her. The author focuses on the moment when fate leads to her discovery by Naoise, which, unbeknownst to her, will lead to the destruction of the finest men of Ulster. Mac na Ceàrdaich's story evinces the state of innocence prior to her discovery;

the relentless workings of fate which leads to her being spotted by Naoise and a premonition of a glorious court being covered in blood.

In the oral tradition, prior to Deirdire's birth Cathbad had prophesised that kings and lords would go to war over her, due to her beauty. She was therefore hidden away and raised by a foster mother. She is, however, discovered by Naoise with whom she eventually elopes, leading to the bloody outcome foretold by Cathbad.

Stylistically, Mac na Ceàrdaich echoes the oral telling of a folk tale in written form by using alliterations, anaphora and other aural techniques. As such these are a literary rendering of an oral phenomenon with the author starting the story with:

> Anns a' **bh**othan **bh**eag am measg nam **b**eann <u>gun fh</u>ios <u>gun fh</u>àth aig duine saoghalta mu dhéidhinn a beò no a coltais bha Deirdire [...].
> (*DMNC*, p. 377, alliterations highlighted)

> *In the small shack amongst the hills, without word or worldy men wise to her life or her appearance, was Deirdire [...].*

Thematically Deirdire's innocence, both within her as an individual and reflected in how she experiences the outside world as revealed to the reader, is opposed by Fate and its ceaseless search for fulfilment by whatever means available. Fate is initially portrayed with an extended weaving metaphor. This reflects Greek mythology where the Fates weave the thread of each individual's life:

> [...] bha Dàn a' suidheachadh nam fuaintean 'sa chrann-deilbh, agus bha dlùth agus uachdar beatha Dheirdire fo bheachd nan Dùl.
> (*DMNC*, p. 377)

> [...] *Fate was placing the pegs in its warping frame, and the warp and weft of Deirdire's life was under the gaze of the Elements.*

As with the fishing gear in 'Là nan Seachd Sìon' Mac na Ceàrdaich uses the technical terms in what appears a determined effort to use lesser-known vocabulary in context. Within a minoritised language this makes practical sense for a politically committed writer, as one of the impacts of minoritisation is a loss of vocabulary and retreat to limited spheres of use. Whilst island readers of Mac na Ceàrdaich's own background would have been more likely to understand the terms directly, the city-based Celtic Revivalists with whom he collaborated may have had less opportunity to be familiar with these simple machines.

The driving force for Deirdire, which the Fates recognise as much as a reader familiar with the wider story, is Love, again couched in terms of weaving:

> B'e so gu dearbh an dlùth a chuir Dàn a dhèanamh suas nan àireamh. B'e so gu dearbh cuideachd a chuir e 's gach urchair san iomairt, agus air an do bhuail e fa dheòigh buille-nimh ud an t-slinne-chlàir.
> (*DMNC*, p. 377)

> *This was certainly the warp Fate put up to make up the yarn needed. This too was certainly what [Fate] put in each shot of the effort, and on where he eventually landed the weaver's board's poisoned blow.*

Once more Mac na Ceàrdaich is drawing attention at the outset to the impulses driving the story to its tragic ending, as this love would lead Deirdire to elope with Naoise, before they are forced to return to Ireland and meet their deaths.

Fate and Deirdire's innocent understanding of the world are intertwined in Deirdire's thoughts about the relentless movement of the burn. This runs from the hill to the bothy where Deirdire is being raised by Gormshuil. Having received no satisfactory answer as to the reasons for the burn's ceaseless movement Deirdire follows it:

> A shamhradh 's a gheamhradh bha esan a' gabhail an aon rathaid gun mhaille, gun ghruaim, gun sgios. Co as an robh a theachd no c'àite an robh e ag imeachd? Cha do thuig a muime brìgh na ceiste a chaidh a chur oirre iomadh uair, ach bha Deirdire a' gabhail chuige féin seadh sònruichte nach do ghabh i oirre a chur am briathar. Bha a spiorad fo gheasaibh an dàin a bha 'ga stiùradh.
> (*DMNC*, p. 379)

> *Summer and winter he took the same road without delay, without complaint, without fatigue. Where was he coming from or where was he going? Her foster-mother did not understand the meaning of the question that had been asked of her many times, but Deirdire took for herself a special meaning that she could not put into words. Her spirit was under the enchantment of the fate that was leading her.*

The narrative itself begins as Deirdire asks to climb the hills to harvest heather roots, used for kindling. Enraptured by the magnificent scene in which she finds herself, she begins to follow the burn in order to satisfy her curiosity as to its origins. The lochan is described as she would have seen it, influenced by the restricted upbringing she had been enduring:

> Ann an lagan beag uaigneach am fasgadh thrì chnoc thàinig Deirdire ar leatha ma dheireadh gu ceann a seud agus a

> siubhail. B' aoibhneach a gean, agus bu lùthor a ceum nuair mhothaich i do lochan beag soilleir sàmhach 'na laidhe an sguird nan cnocan – 'na shuain. [...] B'e so màthair an t-sruthain thuirt cridhe Dheirdire, oir bha i a-nis a' tuigsinn gu ceart gu'm b'e gaol bu chuspair d'a dhuan [...].
> (*DMNC*, p. 381)

> *In the small lonely hollow under the shade of three hills Deirdire thought she had at last come to the goal of her song and her travels. Her spirit was joyous and her step lively as she noticed the small bright quiet lochan lying under the mantle of the hills – asleep. [...] This is the mother of the burn said Deirdire's heart, as she now truly understood that love was the topic of its song [...].*

Now the burn is understood by Deirdire as representing a babbling song of love. To the reader, having been alerted to love and fate's intertwining, the burn continues to develop as a metaphor for the unceasing movement of fate. Deirdire's curiosity is piqued by the reflections of the sun and sky, and the potential for her to see herself in the lochan.

This central scene at the lochan also foreshadows the turmoil to come. As a symbol of the subconscious the bulk of it is unseen despite a surface familiarity and reflectiveness. When Deirdire first looks into it she notices a butterfly in her hair, which she releases – as though she is unleashing part of herself from her constricted life so far. When she looks back into her reflection a man is over her shoulder who disappears when she turns round, and who is not visible when she looks back at the lochan for a third time. Deirdire is not certain she has been seen, but is utterly disquieted by the man's appearance. She also loses her certainty that she has reached the source of the burn she had initially followed. Returning to the hill she sees two more burns come out of it.

From this vantage she has the premonition of the bloody conflict to come. In agitation she watches the sun and clouds above the loch in order to calm herself. The declining sun illuminates the clouds in golden hues:

> Chunnaic i, ar leatha, m' a coinneamh, caisteal mór, àrd éibhinn, uallach le a bhallaichean flathail aoil ag éirigh os cionn mullach nam beann òr-dhaite.
> (*DMNC*, p. 382)

> *She saw, seemingly in front of her, a great castle: tall, delightful, noble with heroic whitewashed walls rising above the gold-coloured hills.*

The joy of imagining herself in this courtly paradise listening to harpers and feasting does not last. Just as surely as the sun setting:

> Chunnaic i an t-sràid gheal a' tionndadh a dreach gus a bhi dearg – dearg mar fhuil. Chunnaic i binneagan agus baidealan a' chaisteil a' leaghadh air falbh gun fhios carson no c' àite.
> (*DMNC*, p. 382)

> *She saw the white street changing its appearance to red – red like blood. She saw the gables and turrets of the castle melting away not knowing why or where to.*

Mac na Ceàrdaich utilises two meanings of 'baideal' meaning a turret and battlement as well as a pillar of cloud.

Deirdire returns to the lochan to drink from it, before following the stream back to the bothy. This is framed as an acceptance of the fate that is in front of her, concluding the symbol of the burn as relentless fate and the route she has to follow – Deirdire's ideal of love, leading to her and Ulster's destruction.

The contrasts between the paradisal environment, the continual invocation of Fate and its gathering forces and finally the bloody vision of the castles tumbling down make the tale a memorable one. It prefigures 'Uamh an Oir' and 'Lughain Lir' in that Mac na Ceàrdaich is reusing a story that has been told before, but investing it with deeper symbolic meaning and psychological development, in line with his goals for Gaelic literature. It also utilises a tragic framework in the same way as *Crois-Tara!*, with an individual's role in deciding their own affairs as restricted as anywhere in Mac na Ceàrdaich's work. The loss of innocence theme is in itself compelling, but Mac na Ceàrdaich is also utilising Gaelic myth to speak of the bloody destruction of 1917. It is also worth reflecting on the loss of innocence as a theme for the emerging post-Easter Rising literature, as well as the theme of many of the English war poets.

Uamh an Oir (1917) (*The Cave of Gold*)

'Uamh an Oir' is also based on a folk tale, one that had variants in different Hebridean islands. A party including a piper enter the cave to explore it or travel through it but are not seen again, with the occasional exception of a surviving dog and the sound of the pipes or singing of the piper depending on the teller. On one level Mac na Ceàrdaich makes explicit the Piper's journey into the cave as a journey towards eternal truth, and a heroic effort to glimpse the certainty that is denied to everyday existence:

> [...] air chul an doruis uamhasaich ud a tha a' sìor-thoirmeasg
> am briathran balbhe do'r sùilean dealasach aon phlathadh;

aon phriobadh-sùl fhaighinn bho Innis so na Brèige air Tìr ud a' Mhór-ioghnaidh. Eolas an Dàin!
(*DMNC*, p. 391)

[...] *behind that awful door that in mute words forever forbids our eager eyes one glimpse; one peep from this Isle of Lies of that Land of Wonder. Knowledge of Fate!*

This is much in keeping with Mac na Ceàrdaich's vision of creative writing as conveying glimpses of eternal truths. He defends his use of a local tale for a universal subject in the same way he argues in favour of the Gaelic language – even animals esteem their own and Gaels would do well to do likewise:

'S aluinn leis gach creutair a ghin féin – eadhon leis an fheannaig a garrach gorm – agus mar sin is muirneach leinn-ne mac duathara ar meanma féin agus ar cinnich.

'S ann mar sin a thig gu m' chluais thar sheachd ciana nan linn fuaim nan dos agus sian cianail nam pong a' giulain nam briathran mulaid gu m' chridhe:

Mu 'n ruig mise, mu 'n tig mis'
A Uamh an Oir, Uamh an Oir!
(*DMNC*, pp. 391–92)

Every creature finds its own offspring beautiful – even the crow its blue garrow – and in the same way delightful to us are the mystical productions of our own imaginations and that of our people.

It is in that manner that the sound of pipe drones come to my ears over the seven long ages and the plaintive

> *enchantment of the notes bearing the words brings sorrow to my heart:*
>
> *Until I reach, until I come*
> *From the Cave of Gold, the Cave of Gold!*

This introduces the refrain from the traditional song that is said to have been heard from the Cave as the piper disappeared.

The second section of the story commences the narration of the specific event in Barra. Initially, Mac na Ceàrdaich uses personification and anthropomorphism to animate the landscape, and create an atmosphere of unease. Whilst the reader is likely to know the outcome of the venture, Mac na Ceàrdaich's description of the landscape is full of an eery dread, as he uses this personification to project the human experience of fear into the landscape:

> Aig casan Creag-Mìle-Brat bha blianag bheag ghorm a' dol sios cho fada 's a leigeadh an t-eagal dhi an coinneamh na mara, agus gu beul na h-uamha air chòir agus gu'n robh mirc a cubhrige a' tuiteam na 'ghiobagan gorma thairis air a bruaich;
> (*DMNC*, p. 392)

> *At the foot of Creag-Mìle-Brat the small grassy green went down as far as fear permitted it before the sea, and right to the mouth of the cave so that the sweetness of its covering fell as a green fringe over its bank;*

Similarly with the seaweed:

> Thog liaghan a cheann buidhe-ruadh os cionn sùghadh athaiseach an tiurra, ach leis an ath-thilleadh mhoidearra

bhog agus dh' fhalaich e a shùil 'san t-saile mar gu'm fac e rud-eiginn.
(*DMNC*, pp. 392–93)

The oarweed lifted its ruddy-yellow head above the leisurely pull of the tideline, but with the soft returning ebb it wet and hid its eye in the sea as though it had seen something.

Mac na Ceàrdaich uses the same technique on the light and atmosphere to finish setting the scene:

bha'n aon ghlumag mhuirtidh so a' lìonadh beul an fheasgair timchioll Creag-Mìle-Brat ionnan is mar a thachdas manadh na sìorrachd seomar-aire nam marbh.
(*DMNC*, p. 393)

this same sultry gloom filled the evening twilight round Creag-Mìle-Brat in the same way that the portent of eternity smothers the room at a wake.

This use of environmental metaphors, pathetic fallacy and personification would be further developed in 'Lughan Lir'.

As well as written literary devices, Mac na Ceàrdaich continues to use aspects of the oral literature style of 'Canach an t-Sléibhe' and so the rhetorical questions, exclamations and terms of affection for the reader remain as though the tale was being orally performed. This made sense for communities where not everyone had reading abilities in both Gaelic and English.

Compared with Nan Eachainn Fhionnlaigh's version in the local oral tradition,[1] Mac na Ceàrdaich incorporates other

---

[1] MacKinnon's recording for the School of Scottish Studies has been digitised at Tobar an Dualchais: Nan MacKinnon, 'Uamh an Oir', www.tobarandualchais.co.uk/track/27961?l=gd

traditions, imbues the story with symbolic meaning and extends the plot beyond what happens in the cave. Mac na Ceàrdaich follows the basic details of the Piper leading a party into the cave at Gearraidh-Gadhal (*Garrygall*) to explore its extent and see whether it leads all the way under the island. The candles the party are carrying are extinguished as they pass under Loch an Dùin by the drips of the water above.

In order to extend the story past the disappearance of the party Mac na Ceàrdaich introduces Morag, who is both the Piper's love interest and whose perspective the story follows after the party's disappearance into the cave. This allows the reader to contemplate with her the meaning of the events. Following their disappearance into the cave, the words of the Piper's tune follow the horrific trajectory of the song:

> Fiolan fiadhaich a' sior-fhiaradh
> Ann am ghlùin, ann am ghlùin.
> [...]
> 'N taobh 'tha fodham a' sior-lothadh
> Daol am shùil, daol am shùil
>
> (*DMNC*, p. 396)

> *Fierce insects constantly climbing / Up my knee, up my knee. / [...] / The side that's under me always rotting / Beetles in my eyes, beetles in my eyes*

Mac na Ceàrdaich does not embellish the traditional song's words with prose description – rather he is aware of the power of the reader's imagination.

The peaceful ending is his most significant addition to the narrative of the folk tale. Rather than leaving the party's disappearance as an unresolved horror story, in Celtic Revivalist fashion he places the piper in Tìr-nan-Òg, about to enter a Christian paradise. This has the benefit of following his westerly trajectory through the caves, with Tìr-nan-Òg being traditionally described as a mystical land in the West:

> [...] cha b'ann, a ghràidh, fo Loch an Dùin a bha dachaidh 'aisling an comunn na feadhnach a dh' fhalbh. Cha b' ann gu dearbh, ach fada, fada ás a sin, seachad air Aird Ghrìnn, agus seachad air Tìr-fo-Thuinn, thall, fada thall an iomall Torra Domhainn ann an Tìr-nan-Òg.
> (*DMNC*, p. 397)

> [...] *it wasn't, my love, under Loch an Dùin that his home was, dreaming amongst those who departed. It wasn't indeed, but far far from there, past Aird Grein and past the Land-Under-Waves, far over at the edge of Torra Domhainn in Tìr-nan-Òg.*

Sitting high above the Atlantic looking West, a view described as 'dearbh choimeas na Siorrachd' (*DMNC*, p. 397) ('*the very likeness of eternity*'), Morag glimpses her lover playing his instrument whilst perambulating a red mountain. At its peak is the Marian image of the Mother and Infant, who has a golden globe in his hand:

> Có a tha siod 'na seasamh air mullach a' chnuic chrà-dheirg 's a h-éideadh de liath nam flathas? 'Na h-asgaill tha Leanabh aig am bheil ball òir 'na Làimh. Tha 'n cnoc a' gluasad agus 'g a' sior-thogail suas. Air a cùlaobh tha dorus mórail deth 'm bheil gathan grian-gheal agus tha a làmh dheas-se a' seòladh a' phiobaire ga ionnsuigh!
> (*DMNC*, p. 397)

> *Who is that standing on the summit of the blood red hill and her garments a heavenly blue? In her arms is an Infant with a golden orb in his Hands. The hill is moving and ever rising*

> *upwards. Behind her is a great door giving off rays of sunlight-white and her right hand steers the piper towards it!*

Morag responds in kind with a prayer which is taken up by the birds. This is in Alexander Carmichael's *Carmina Gadelica* mould. She alludes to the Marian title Gate of Heaven, and Mac na Ceàrdaich completes this restoration of calm using the birds, contrasting with the earlier dread evinced by the natural world:

> Chrom Morag a ceann – oir thuig i. 'Fàilt ort, a Ghrianain Oir! Beannaicheam dhuit, a Dhoruis Fhlathanais!' Thog eòin an t-sléibhe na facail o a beul agus luaidh iad a' leadan le fonn.
> (*DMNC*, p. 398)

> *Morag bowed her head – for she understood. 'Welcome, Golden Light! Bless you, Door of Paradise!' The birds of the muir took up the words from her mouth and spread the litany with joy.*

Mac na Ceàrdaich has achieved an important composite of traditional folk narrative, Christian belief and Celtic Revivalism, advancing in particular the range of techniques being used to develop atmosphere in the Gaelic short story. In 1917, these concerns with life after death were of importance not just in the trenches but in the post-Rising centre of the Celtic Revival in Dublin. The Celtic Revival imagery in an explicit Catholic guise is very much in keeping with his poetic compositions from the same period. The following year, in his anti-war essay 'Innis-na-Brèige', Mac na Ceàrdaich is more adamant that eternal truths can only occasionally be glimpsed from this world – reaching them is an altogether more complicated matter.

Lughain Lir (1921) (*The Powers of the Sea*)
Mac na Ceàrdaich's development of the short story form reaches its peak in 'Lughain Lir' (*DMNC*, pp. 399–421). In this work, we see a further elaboration of the literary techniques he had honed in 'Uamh an Oir': using anthropomorphism, pathetic fallacy and symbolism to describe the landscapes and characters simultaneously, skilfully merging the landscape and themes being explored. This interweaving of the natural world with the psychological worlds of the characters allows him to develop themes familiar from his 1915–16 long poem 'Là nan Seachd Sìon', of the mariner as a prophetic poet and moments of crisis being portrayed at sea.

'Lughain Lir' is the longest of Mac na Ceàrdaich's short stories, and is structured in eight sections. The first four introduce the characters on shore and culminate with a fishing boat's departure from Bagh-an-Eilean after the report of herring in Loch Fada. The primary character Dòmhnull Mac Eoin / An t-Eun (*Donald Johnston / The Bird*) is skipper of An Òigh (*The Maiden*), and strikes up a grandfatherly bond with his widowed neighbour's son. Mac Eòin's wife, daughter and son-in-law Eachainn, who is a crew member aboard Dòmhnull's boat alongside another named character Calum, are also introduced in these sections. The final four sections look at the crew's time at sea and their attempts to return home in time for Christmas. These culminate with An Òigh's return to port after much adversity, as a result of both human folly and the elemental hardship of the sea in winter.

Structurally Mac-na-Ceàrdaich's story is an advent narrative of trial and tribulation running from just after St Andrew's day until the eventual joyful reunification at midnight on Christmas morning. Dòmhnull fulfils his promise to return bearing a Christmas gift for the fatherless boy; as well as seeing his own family unit reunited and meeting his new grandson.

Mac na Ceàrdaich layers the religious imagery of his story, combining more universal Catholic theology with traditional Hebridean devotions. The intercessionary role of Mary is alluded to near the beginning and end of the work. In the first instance, he is quieting the widow's son's distress as his model boat is caught in a current taking it out towards the open seas. An t-Eun says his own ship An Òigh will bring the model back to shore:

> 'A dheoin Dia,' 's e a fhreagair e, 'tillidh, oir cha do dhiùlt Ise riamh iarrtas dian a' chridhe naoidheanta.'
> Ach na'n robh de thuigse aig a' phàisde mhothaicheadh e neul eile air gnùis an 'Eoin,' agus ma thuig e o bhlas nam facal nach b'ann ris féin a bha 'n corr de bhriathran Dhòmhnuill Mhic Eoin, bha e riaraichte leis na thuig e gu ceart, oir bha e cinnteach gu'm b'fhior na thubhairt, gu'm b'fhior a thilleadh, seadh, a dheòin Dia, a dheòin na h-Oighe. (*DMNC*, p. 401)

> *'By God's will,' was how he answered, 'She'll return it, as She never rejected a child's heart's fervent wish.'*
> *But if the child had enough understanding he would have noticed another light on An t-Eun's face, and if he understood from the manner of speaking that the rest of Donald Johnston's words weren't addressed to him, he was satisfied with what he had understood correctly, as he was certain that what was said was true, that the [the model's] return was true, yes, by God's will, by the Maiden's will.*

This confidence in Marian intercession was an important fact of Southern Hebridean life. The characters themselves have varying degrees of awareness of the allegory being created. An t-Eun grows aware as he speaks that he is combining his intention to retrieve the model himself using his ship the Maiden, with the role of the Virgin Mary in interceding as a result of the fervent prayers of the faithful. This motif is repeated in the final section when the widow's son asks his mother about the role of Mary in intercession and petitionary prayer. Reassured by her answers he is confident that An t-Eun will return, with a new caman (*shinty stick*) as promised.

It's not just Marian intercession that is crucial to the narrative, Mac na Ceàrdaich utilises the names of the fishing fleet again with 'An Òigh' ('*The Maiden*') and An t-Eun's brother-in-law's ship the 'Reul na Maidne' ('*The Morning Star*'). The latter Marian title adds to the advent feel of a moment of joy to come, as a symbol of the dawn arriving. Mac na Ceàrdaich also refers to the molucca beans that periodically wash up on the West Coast far from their Caribbean origins, known as the cnò Mhoire, which were commonly retained as household Marian symbols, due to their having a cross on them. One of these is given to an t-Eun by the boy for returning his model boat to him; it is crushed in an t-Eun's hand at a climactic moment as he lunges overboard to save one of his crew.

Mac na Ceàrdaich uses an t-Eun to explore the image of the mariner as visionary and truth-teller that also occurs in 'Là nan Seachd Sìon'. We are informed early in the story that he received his nickname as a result of his resemblance to the annlag-mhara or storm petrel. This bird had featured in European literature as a harbinger of storm and deaths, connected with Mother Carey, wife of Davy Jones. In section VII an t-Eun encounters a petrel in his dream, awakening to find the fishing boat in imminent danger. An t-Eun is recognised as the last of 'na daoine' – which is literally '*the people*', but signifies his status within the community. In his case it is as the last of a generation of seafarers who were reliant entirely on wind power; their own knowledge and ability to navigate. He alone notes the approaching storm in the brindled cloud formations to the north, in language echoing section III of 'Là nan Seachd Sìon':

> Cha b'ann gun fhios no gun aire do Dhòmhnull Mac Eoin a bha aon de chomharran Nàduir a' deanamh frìth nam fios, oir b'ann dha féin a b' aithne a leabhar a leughadh gu ceart. B'ann leis-san gun teagamh a bha an t-eòlas agus an tuigse air nach do ruig leabhar a' mhic-leughainn; eòlas agus tuigse air oidheam nan dùl agus air cridhe sean duathara na mara. B' esan 'na aonar de sgiobadh na h-'Òigh' air nach robh fonn nam fiughair oir bu smuaireanach a choltas is e 'na shuidhe mar a b' àbhaist aig an stiùir.
> (*DMNC*, p. 410)

> *It didn't go unnoticed or unheeded by Dòmhnull Mac Eoin what one of Nature's marks was auguring, as he was able to read its book correctly. He had, without doubt, the knowledge and understanding that was reached by no scholar's book; a knowledge and understanding of the elements' tutor and of the old mystical heart of the sea. He alone of the crew of the 'Maiden' was not in high spirits of expectation, as his appearance was somewhat melancholic sitting as usual at the helm.*

Nature has left its mark on an t-Eun as well. In describing his relationship with the generations of young boys who live around the bay, Mac na Ceàrdaich uses one of his many animal similes:

> B'e sin an t-èun, mar na lach eile, a thug teagasg iomchuidh do na h-àil sin agus a rinn cuideachd iomadh éiginn a chur féin as leth am beatha, a mànrain agus am faoin-iarrtasan.
> (*DMNC*, p. 400)

That was the bird, like the other sea fowl, that gave a proper education to that brood and who also took many strifes upon himself on behalf of their sustenance, their cries and their petty wishes.

In this way descriptions of the natural world and characters overlap throughout the story, with one being used to describe the other:

Dha-san bha an tonn a' cheart cho dualach 's a bha e do isean an ròin, is cha robh beo a chuireadh sgaradh eatorra. Ged a chaidh a bhreith air tìr, cha robh tìr dha ach mar chreig an anmoich do'n èun mhara; cha robh fìor neo fìreanneach dha ach saoghal saor a chuain – guth na mara a bha gach là ag ath-aithris 'na chluasan iorram agus agallamh a sheanaran.
(*DMNC*, p. 403)

To him the wave was as natural as it was to a seal pup, and there were none alive who would separate them. Even though he was born on dry land, land was just the same to him as the night rock to a sea bird; there was no realness nor reality to him aside from the free world of the sea – the voice of the sea that was every day repeating the rowing songs and chatter of his ancestors.

This is a two-way process, with animals, the sea and the island all being given human qualities as well. This is initially used for mood setting, as in 'Uamh an Oir':

[...] bha gart seang agus néul ciar an ràithe air laighe air na gàirdeanan loma cnuachdach a bha 'ga sìneadh féin mu thimchioll Bàgh-an-Eilean.
(*DMNC*, p. 399)

> [...] *the threatening gaunt aspect and gloomy hues of the season had lain on the bare, lumpen arms that were stretching themselves around Bàgh-an-Eilean.*

This interplay between man and nature takes on an ethical dimension when Mac na Ceàrdaich shows the various ways the crew react to the trials facing them at sea. Contrasting with an t-Eun's nautical ability, steadfastness and commitment to reach Bàgh-an-Eilean, Eachainn Mhìcheil is tempted by material reward and Calum despairs of ever reaching home. Eachainn Mhìcheil's casting of the nets initially looks like it will reap a financial benefit for the whole crew but imperils the crew to the extent that the fifteen nets are cut adrift. Similarly, Calum is initially disturbed by an t-Eun's order to open the compass and help measure the boat's speed using the log to calculate the knots at which she is proceeding. Mac na Ceàrdaich's narrator relays to the readers the anxious questions he asks himself:

> An robh fhios aig an "Eun" c' àite an robh iad? An robh fhios aige cho trom 's a bha an sgoth – seadh agus cho sean 's a bha i? Nach robh gach maothan a bha 'na corp a' fuasgladh? Nach robh gach ball bodhaige a beairte dhi air chrith cho luath ris an duilleach air a' chraoibh?
> (*DMNC*, p. 416)
>
> *Did an t-Eun know where they were? Did he know how heavily laden the boat was – aye, and how old she was? Was not every sheet of her unravelling? Was not every line of the rigging shaking as swift as the leaves of tree?*

Hearing one of the masts breaking behind him, Calum believes the boat to have split in two and casts himself overboard only to be rescued by an t-Eun.

The despair and greed of the crewmates contrasts with an t-Eun who recognises the predicament immediately on awakening, piloting the ship to safety by unhesitatingly rejecting the worldliness of Eachainn Mhìcheil and disgarding the catch and nets. An t-Eun's commitment to returning as promised is clearly evidenced in VI and VII, where we learn it was his decision to leave the fishery early on Christmas Eve and return to Bàgh-an-Eilean as fast as possible. Mac na Ceàrdaich's contrast between the worldliness of Eachann Mhìcheil and the principles of an t-Eun keeping his promise to the widow's son explores a theme from his very first published poem 'Faoileag an Droch Chladaich' ('*The Gull of the Poor Shore*') where the poet considers the advantages of economic progress versus contentment in your home community. But it also shows the role of the poetic visionary with right understanding in informing ethical behaviour.

As well as exploring Marian themes, truth and ethics, and the power of obligations, 'Lughan Lìr' is a supreme imaginative depiction of the Gaelic herring fisherman of the late nineteenth and early twentieth centuries. Mac na Ceàrdaich's life until he left for Edinburgh was dominated by this trade: not only had he worked in it, as had his brothers, but his father's livelihood and the family income was entirely dependent on the success of the herring fishery. Mac na Ceàrdaich uses the real names of vessels that sailed from Castlebay during the period, and the singing and piping crew member Calum could well be based on his cousin and one-time flatmate Calum Johnston, who also made the transition from fisherman to electrical engineer. Perhaps more importantly, however, it retains an important role as one of the earliest modern short stories in Gaelic: with a range of technique and depth of character development that makes it distinct from many of the tales of previous writers.

5. INBHE AR BÀRDACHD (1916) (*THE DEVELOPMENT OF OUR POETRY*)

The essay 'Inbhe ar Bàrdachd' (*DMNC*, pp. 332–341) is the closest Mac na Ceàrdaich comes to a poetic manifesto. There had not previously been much published material dedicated to finding a basis from which to critique Gaelic poetry and on which to create new literature. This essay is Mac na Ceàrdaich's response to that situation and provides an insight in to his novel thinking when it came to the poetry of his predecessors. The basis he proposed for both critiquing and developing Gaelic poetry is the same idealistic vision of revealing eternal truths to the audience, that the mariner symbolises in 'Lughain Lir' and 'Là nan Seachd Sion'.

Published in 1916, contemporaneously with 'Là nan Seachd Sion', the fact that Mac na Ceàrdaich's topic is held to be innovative is demonstrated most clearly by the introductory paragraphs. As if starting a traditional poetic epic he refers to the Muses but stresses that he has not been inspired by them to provide definitive statements on the matter but rather:

> [...] mar aon neach a tha a' gabhail de dhanadas air an cead-san aidmheil a chridhe a dhèanamh folaiseach do thaobh Ealain aosda is urramach air na chuir a shinnsir meas agus luach.
> (*DMNC*, p. 332)

> [...] *as one who has taken enough boldness by their leave to make clear the creed of his heart on this old and honorouble art, valued and esteemed by our forbears.*

This is contrasted with those who believed that it's best not to speak too much on something of such importance, or indeed, who prefer praising rather than criticising: '[...] an duan a mholas gach nì 's nach toir iomradh air ann-tlachd; an aon duan 's a bha Nero eile a' seinn 's an Ròimhe 'na teine' (*DMNC*, p. 332) ('[...] *the song that praises everything and does not refer to displeasure; the same song that another Nero sang as Rome burned*').

The distaste for criticism that Mac na Ceàrdaich is referring to in the wider public should not be assumed to be necessarily a feature of Gaelic literature alone. Popular criticism in English was still heavily influenced by the historical method – poet's biographies were held to be a main interpretative guide for criticism. This was also true in Gaelic literature, where the nineteenth-century anthology *Sàr-Obair nam Bàrd Gaelach* (*The Beauties of Gaelic Poetry*) had a short biographical sketch for each poet, or in Uilleam MacDhunlèibhe's 1882 collection, where Robert Blair's introductory remarks include anecdotes about the poet's life rather than significant engagement with the texts. Practical Criticism and the type of close reading familiar to school pupils today were not yet the ubiquitous forms of analysis they have now become. Indeed, this process of looking at the effects of component parts of a poem was at the time dismissed in some quarters as an autopsy-like dismembering of a poem's organic whole.

Mac na Ceàrdaich's quest for a more satisfying basis for both the production and criticism of Gaelic poetry addresses an increasingly pressing need; especially if the poetry was to be able to span the whole range from popular song to prose poems. But this also emerges as a result of the change of the production and transmission of Gaelic poetry. Much criticism in the oral tradition worked in a negative way; unpopular poems were simply forgotten or adapted if an insufficient number of listeners were willing to reperform them. Published poetry, where new poetry is required to ensure people would buy the publication, operated differently in that it required originality. This in turn leads to Mac na Ceàrdaich's question – if it is to be based on more than passing fashion, what should be the basis of the new poetry?

The form this basis takes is Mac na Ceàrdaich's aesthetic reaction to the chaos of the First World War. In defending his idealist conception of poetry Mac na Ceàrdaich says:

> Seallamaid air clàr na h-Eorpa truaighe an diugh agus gabhamaid leasan. Fhuair nithealachd choirbte aonta fhada air cathair Ceartais feadh 's a bha Spiorad na Fìrinn fo 'n chois, agus ar leam gur dall an neach nach aidich gur e dubh agus salach buil a riaghlaidh.
> (*DMNC*, p. 341)

> *Let us look across wretched Europe today and take a lesson. Corrupted materialism had a lengthy lease on the throne of Justice whilst the Spirit of Truth was trod underfoot, and blind is the man who won't admit that black and filthy are the consequences of its rule.*

The failure of the civilising role of literature, that nineteenth-century educators believed would lead to humanity's improvement, was all too clear.

As in a number of his other essays Mac na Ceàrdaich's language is of a deliberately high register, in contrast with his popular songs and comedies. Archaic forms such as 'do thaobh' (more usually 'a thaobh') appear throughout. These had been fossilised in the Gaelic of nineteenth-century bibles which had a significant impact on formal styles of Gaelic. This combined with the lengthy multi-clause sentences and abstractions such as the Muses and Art makes the essay deliberately more challenging than much of the other Gaelic prose of the period. This in turn suggests Mac na Ceàrdaich is forming an argument as to the nature and prospects for Gaelic poetry that is aimed at other poets and critics as opposed to a general audience.

To structure his argument Mac na Ceàrdaich builds from first principles, as he does in other essays.[1] He describes this process as 'reusonachadh purpail' (pointed or sound reasoning) as he looks to build an *a priori* argument. This is a deliberate move to test and if necessary replace the insecure chauvinistic certainties about the superiority of Gaelic verse with an argument about how best the literature should develop: 'teagamh a chur 'nar beachd féin car greiseige air chòir is gu'n dearbh sinn dhuinn féin le reusonachadh purpail gu bheil sinn da rìribh air slighe na fìrinne' (*DMNC*, p. 333) (*'doubt our opinion awhile, so that we can prove to ourselves with sound reasoning that we are on the path of truth'*).

For all he was looking to maintain a Gaelic and Scottish identity he is not anglophobic in his literary inspiration and aspirations. Elsewhere he speaks of the need for the Gaelic community to consider its own state and consciousness but 'Inbhe ar Bàrdachd' praises English literature throughout, and uses Shakespeare and Pope to establish the yardstick for the comparison between the two literatures. The ability to convey truths to the wider public is the role of the poet, and English literature is compared favourably to Gaelic poetry in this regard. His references to Scots and English-language poetry runs from John Barbour to Robert Bridges, then Poet Laureate.

In a Gaelic context, particularly for a poet who continued to compose songs for both popular performance and publication, Mac na Ceàrdaich's relative dismissal of the rhythmic and aural aspects of poetry is significant. Later critics, especially Sorley MacLean and Derick Thomson, would use their own yardsticks such as realism and originality to condemn

---

[1] Such as his 1916 analysis of the situation of the Gaelic language community 'A' Ghàidhlig agus a Muinntir' (DMNC, pp. 319–31) ('Gaelic and her People').

some of what had previously been considered the Gaelic canon. Similarly, in Mac na Ceàrdaich's idealistic view the words should be regarded as empty vessels:

> Cha'n iad na briathran susbaint no bladh an eòlais bhàrdail, oir cha'n eil gu dearbh na briathran ach mar shoithichean a' giulain an eòlais gu ruige ar tuigse-ne.
> (*DMNC*, p. 334)

> *The words are not the substance or essence of poetic knowledge, as these words are but the vessels carrying knowledge towards our ken.*

Mac na Ceàrdaich is aware of how problematic his argument is in a Gaelic literary context. His argument leads to the condemnation of 'Moladh Beinn Dòrain', one of the most widely praised eighteenth-century Gaelic long poems, on the grounds that Donnchadh Bàn Mac an t-Saoir (*Duncan Macintyre*) praised the hind and the hunt but Beinn Dòrain is without praise yet: 'Fhuair an eilid agus an t-seilg am moladh, ach tha Beinn-Dòrain gun mholadh fhathast' (*DMNC*, p. 336). The runs of adjectives that would later exasperate Derick Thomson are therefore also rejected as superflous.

This subjugating of the aural aspects of poetry to its inherent meaning opens Mac na Ceàrdaich up to free verse and prose poems. These feature in his experiments with symbolist essays: 'Mar sin, tuigidh sinn nach eil e idir uile-riatanach rannta-chadh a bhi air na briathran bàrdail ged a tha e ionmhuinn leis a' chluais' (*DMNC*, p. 334) ('*As such, we understand that it isn't entirely mandatory to versify poetic words even though it is dear to the ear*').

Mac na Ceàrdaich would experiment in this direction using prose for non-narrative and poetic pieces starting with 'Gaol-Aoibhneas' ('*Love-Joy*') (*DMNC*, pp. 384–86) and 'Gaol-Mhulad' ('*Love-Grief*') (*DMNC*, pp. 387–90) in 1917 and also 1927's 'Dealachadh nan Rathad' ('*The Parting of the Ways*') (*DMNC*, pp. 426–31).

Mac na Ceàrdaich elaborates fully on his prophetic vision of poetry. The poet's role is described as being:

> [...] staid spioradail agus cheud-fathach, agus, maraon, chorporra, a cho-chreutairean a thogail á otraich na diblidheachd, agus an seòladh le lòchran a sholuis gu mullach nam Beanntan Siorruidh ud air a bheil Soillse na Dearbh-Fhìrinn a' dealradh gu bràth.
> (*DMNC*, p. 338)

> [...] *to lift the spiritual and intellectual, as well as bodily, state of his fellow creatures out of the midden of wretchedness, and steer them with the light of his lamp to the summit of those Eternal Mountains where the Light of Truth shines eternal.*

This is not the rejection of worldly matter and concerns that it immediately appears to be as Mac na Ceàrdaich says: 'Tha a h-uile nì a' laomadh; a' cur thairis le brigh is ciallachadh' (*DMNC*, p. 339) ('*Everything is overflowing with meaning and significance*'). As is clear in his poem 'An Dùradan Duslaich' ('*The Speck of Dust*'), Mac na Ceàrdaich believes the meanest material can have a universal significance.

For all the prophetic and idealist imagery Mac na Ceàrdaich's concluding proposal can be summarised as: Gaelic poetry should be reorganised in a way that prioritises truth and reflects its Celtic origins. Again using the comparison with English literature:

> [...] seallamaid gu dè an call agus a' bhochduinn a thigeadh air litreachas an t-Sasunnaich nan tigeadh na seann

Ghreugaich, agus iomadh dream eile a thoirt air falbh leo nan 'clachan snaidhte' sin a shlad an Sasunnach [...] a thogail nan aitreabhan bàrdail a tha ri 'ainm an diugh.
(*DMNC*, p. 340)

[...] *consider the loss and poverty that would befall English literature if the the old Greeks and many other people arrived to take away the marbles that the Englishman plundered* [...] *to build the palaces of poetry they have to their name today.*

Gaelic has its distinctive ancient tradition and that should be used to build the foundations of the new poetry, in keeping with the ideals of the Celtic Revival then well underway. In Mac na Ceàrdaich's terms this is the '"Blas Ceilteach": leis a bheil mi a' ciallachadh seann-aidmheil agus seann-seanachas ar cinnich' (*DMNC*, p. 340) ('*"A Celtic Flavour": by which I mean the ancient creeds and ancient folklore of our people*').

Both Mac na Ceàrdaich's own writing and the more well-known Sorley MacLean's 'Dàin do Eimhir', a collection of poems to a legendary Irish heroine, would suggest that this approach of a fearless dedication to truth and repurposing aspects of earlier Gaelic literature was to be a fruitful one.

6. POETRY

Mac na Ceàrdaich first composed poems and songs at school, a practice he continued after moving to Edinburgh. He was first published in *Guth na Bliadhna* in 1913, and continued to write poetry up to his death in 1932. His poetry shares the wide range of subjects and forms seen in his prose and drama: songs both traditional and stylised, lyrics, dialogues and translations. Whilst his interests in nature and theology make repeated appearances, he also explores social commentary, philosophical reflection and political incitement. The mixture of styles means that rather than having a singular poetic voice a number of formal approaches are used, in which similar themes emerge. This variation is further reflected in the linguistic choices he makes, moving from the accessible language of the humorous songs to more archaic and high-register Gaelic in more stylised printed lyric poetry.

One of the earliest themes that emerges in his poetry, and then remains throughout, is the conflicted desire for personal financial security whilst wanting to remain part of a community; particularly how this is encapsulated by the crisis decision to emigrate. Whilst the number of Gaelic songs by emigrants is plentiful, Mac na Ceàrdaich approaches the theme differently using lyrics and poetic dialogues as well as songs in a high register to explore the topic. Songs by city-based Gaels in praise of their respective homelands were later somewhat derided, but he does not appear to look down on these shared communal recollections. These songs used codified visual imagery and place names to permit the audience to envisage landscapes far from their present surroundings. Rather he explores other approaches to the same themes, whilst also being willing to develop more familiar tropes.

His first published poem **'Faoileag an Droch-Chladaich'** (*'The Gull of the Poor Shore'*) (*DMNC*, pp. 31–32) appeared in *Guth na Bliadhna* in 1913, and is a dialogue between a Fisherman and the eponymous gull. It is the first of two poetic dialogues Mac na Ceàrdaich writes featuring a conversation with a natural entity using a higher register of Gaelic. The use of dialogues was a periodic feature of vernacular Gaelic poetry. Earlier examples include the late sixteenth-century Dòmhnall Mac Fhionnlaigh nan Dàn's 'Òran na Comhachaig' (*'The Song of the Owl'*)[1] that features a dialogue between a hunter and an ancient owl. Iain Dall MacAoidh (*John MacKay*) personified Coire an Easain in his song to that corrie in the late seventeenth century.

Like his predecessors, Mac na Ceàrdaich believes in a wisdom in nature, 'eòlas nàdair', as he demonstrates in 'Faoileag'. Whilst this was common in nineteenth-century romantic verse, Mac na Ceàrdaich's natural wisdom reflects a range of influences. In some cases, as with 'Là nan Seachd Sìon', this wisdom is presented in a Catholic guise, leading to echoes of a medieval system of Christian signs being found in the book of nature. However, both 'Faoileag an Droch-Chladaich' and 'Creag nan Sgarbh' (*'The Cormorants' Rock'*) (*DMNC*, p. 37) are more broadly philosophical works, rather than explicitly religious. Both have a young man struggling to understand or express his thoughts, and the tension is resolved by the encounter with the personified natural entity.

In 'Faoileag', the young fisherman is not the image of foresight and wisdom that the mariner will be in 'Là nan Seachd Sìon'. Rather, like Eachainn in 'Lughain Lir', his concerns are more prosaic and indeed show a lack of understanding:

---

[1] McLeod and Bateman, *Duanaire na Sracaire: Songbook of the Pillagers – an Anthology of Scotland's Gaelic Verse to 1600* (Birlinn, 2007), pp. 392–404.

Innis **dhomh**, oir dh'fhairtlich **orm**,
Dé 'tha thu '**lorg** a <u>bhuannachd as</u>,
'S nach fhaic mo *shùil* ach cladach **borb**
A' *fùid*each' **colg** nan <u>stuaghannan</u>.
(DMNC, p. 31, rhyme-scheme highlighted)[1]

Tell me, as it baffles me / What benefit you find in it, / As my eyes see nought but barbarous shore / Dispersing the wrath of the breakers.

In fact, it is the gull who is held up as the old wise figure in this poem and its reply emphasises both the lack of vision of the fisherman, and humanity as a whole:

Ar leam, 'ill' òig, gur plaoisg do ghlóir
Is nach eil eólas nàduir leat,
'S ged 's mór do chòir-s' air aithne chòrr,
Nach eil do chomhairl' ro thàbhachdach.
Ged tha mo bhòrd-sa lom de lòn
'An sùilean sòghail àrd-bhithean;
Tha mise, fòs, gun dìth gun bhròn
Is m' inntinn stòld' is sàthaichte.
(DMNC, pp. 31–32)

I believe, young boy, your cry rings hollow / And you do not have nature's wisdom with you, / Though great's your access to wider knowledge / Your advice is not so profitable. / Though my table is bare of food and ware / In the eyes of decadent

---

[1] As well as summarising the poet's confusion, the excerpt shows the complex rhyme scheme used throughout Mac na Ceàrdaich's poetry. While a deeper analysis of this is beyond the scope of this work, the aural aspects of the poetry in terms of internal rhyme, end-rhyme and assonance should be borne in mind, when reading the translations.

higher creatures; / I am, still, without want nor care / My mind settled and satisfied.

The fundamental contrast between contentment and desire for advancement has a geographical basis in Mac na Ceàrdaich's life between the island and the city. The ending of each half of the stanza, the rhyming dactyls 'thàbhachdach' (*'profitable'*) and 'sàthaichte' (*'satisfied'*), emphasise this contrast. For a nature poem, Mac na Ceàrdaich's use of more pecuniary terminology evinces a more material mood throughout the poem: 'stàth' (*'use/profit'*) at the last stress of the first line; 'socair-shògh' (*'leisurely luxury'*); 'solar' (*'procure'*) and 'soirbh' (*'easy/prosperous'*).

This debate on economic progress versus contentment is most explicit in the good-natured **'Oran air Deifir Beachd'** (*'A Song on a Difference of Opinion'*) (*DMNC*, pp. 124–26), which is also in dialogue form. Mac na Ceàrdaich puts forward the proposition that his fellow Barrach Donald MacAskill and he would be better off had they stayed in Barra, by drawing on the pastoral beauty of the landscapes of their youth. MacAskill responds by saying that the poet is failing by not considering his subject fully. Bringing a cold dose of reality to the debate he highlights Mac na Ceàrdaich's failings as a fisherman and the hardship of that life, leading to the conclusion that they are indeed better off in Edinburgh drinking bitter pints.

The contrast between contentment in nature and desire to progress financially is evident in one of Mac na Ceàrdaich's most popular lyrics, successful both as a remarkable written poem and widely adopted song **'Loch na h-Ob'** (*DMNC*, pp. 40–41). Written in praise of the loch at the North East of Barra where his brother Niall, whom Mac na Ceàrdaich would visit in the summer, was a Schoolmaster at Sgoil a' Mhorghain (*North Bay School*), this poem likewise frames the beauty of the loch in the context of urban reminiscing.

The opening image of a sunbeam entering a dark room on a May morning, and its comparison with the memory of the loch coming into the poet's mind, leads to an abundance of praise for the loch and its surrounding flora and fauna. By starting with the sunbeam simile, which is subsequently revealed to be of a memory, which is then only revealed to be of the Loch in the final words of the eight-line stanza, Mac na Ceàrdaich successfully toys with the anticipation of the reader, paralleling his own desire for the Loch in contrast with the suddenness of the memory's arrival. But the idyll is one of remembrance in contrast with everyday life's strife and stresses and there is an underlying anxiety named at the end of the poem that this idyll too can be corrupted, as well as the city-based unhappiness that makes him yearn for the loch, as captured in the sixth stanza.

The poem builds from the initial sunbeam images with carefully constructed stanzas and a refrain of 'Loch na h-Ob' at the end of each one. For example, two stanzas use anaphora and parallel structures to build up layers of imagery, only for the refrain to make clear that the loch's beauty remains supreme:

> Cha'n ioghnadh sruthan beinn an *fhraoich*
> 'Bhi ruith le *caoin*-ghuth **cheòl**;
> Cha'n ioghnadh bradan mear nan *caol*
> 'Bhi leumnaich *ao*trom **òg**;
> Cha'n ioghnadh leam an fhaoileag <u>bhàn</u>
> Le 'gaol a' <u>snàmh</u> gu *fòill*;
> Oir 's sonas uile dhaibh gu <u>bràth</u>
> 'Bhi <u>tàmh</u> an Loch na h-**Ob**.
>
> (*DMNC*, p. 41)

No wonder the heather hill's burn / Runs with softly sung tune; / No wonder the narrows' lively salmon / Is leaping lightly youthfully; / No wonder the fair herring gull / Lovingly swims at ease; / For happiness is theirs for ever / Abiding in Loch na h-Ob.

As well as the repetition of the 'Cha'n ioghnadh' for the opening of the first three couplets, the eight-line stanzas have an intricate rhyme scheme, which has been highlighted in the above excerpt. The ò rhyme runs throughout the seven stanzas leading to the use of the poetic and archaic 'lò' in place of 'là' as the final word of the poem. However, the syntax of the poem remains generally straightforward, with the clauses matching the linebreaks as in the example above.

Having layered images of natural and heavenly beauty in the first five stanzas, Mac na Ceàrdaich changes tone suddenly in the penultimate stanza with the declaratory statement about life's woes contrasting with 'sonas' (*'happiness'*) and 'tàmh' (*'reside/at peace'*) in the previous couplet:

> 'Se cor na beatha dragh is streup,
> 'S an cois an streup thig bròn,
> [...]
> An uair bhios smalan agus gruaim
> A' dubhadh duairc mo neòil,
> Gheibh m' anam sonas, fois, is cluain
> An uaigneas Loch na h-Ob.
>
> (*DMNC*, p. 41)

Life's lot is worry and strife / Behind the strife comes grief, / [...] / When sorrow and gloom / Darken my hue's frown / My spirit takes happiness, rest and peace / In the solitude of Loch na h-Ob.

You can see how the poet also uses repetition of streup *strife* and end-line emphasis on streup and bròn *grief* to create this blunt change of tone. Whilst the majority of the poem is on the beauty of the loch, after the initial sunbeam in a dark room image, this sixth stanza and the fear of corruption mentioned in passing in the final verse, make clear to the reader the complexity of the exile's relationship with the beauty of his home. In this poem, however, the mental image of the Loch wins out, and the peace-of-mind mentioned is granted to the exiled poet, leading to the exuberant final stanza.

Overall Mac na Ceàrdaich creates a finely crafted poem in a high register which is still accessible to a general audience. Its simple imagery and vocabulary can perhaps disguise the formal elements: parallelisms; the sudden opening on a simile; the anticipation built up to the refrain in each verse and the changes of tone for the sixth and seventh stanzas. This combination of intricacy and accessibility makes it one of his most successful poetic works, from a formal and popular perspective.

Mac na Ceàrdaich does not only remember in exile, he returns with songs about city life and writes poems for those who feel forced to leave. His song **'Fàilte do Bharraidh'** (*'Welcome to Barra'*) (*DMNC*, pp. 121–23) replicates a ship's approach to Castlebay, the port on Barra, with stanzas marking the stages of the approach to the island up until disembarking. Mac na Ceàrdaich captures the joy and anticipation of returning to the island community after a year away working and a long voyage from Oban, concluding with him being welcomed ashore. Whilst the song could well have been performed in the cèilidh atmosphere which helped pass the journey, Mac na Ceàrdaich draws out some of the same psychological contrasts at work in Loch na h-Ob:

> 'S e bhi toirt mu chùlthaobh
> Ri baile mór na smùide

Rinn m' aigneadh chur ri sùgradh
'S thog gach smùr bhar m' aire-sa.

(*DMNC*, p. 121)

It's turning my back / On the city of smoke / That's turned my spirits to merriment / And lifted each woe from my mind.

This joyful perspective is reversed in his song **'A' Bheannachd Bharrach'** (*'The Barra Blessing'*) (*DMNC*, pp. 86–87) which shows Mac na Ceàrdaich using the mixture of Celtic Revival and religious imagery in his poetry that was also so stimulating to his prose writing. This was written for the emigrants who left Barra bound for Canada in March 1924. It appeared in *Guth na Bliadha*, published with a Celtic-designed capital B. Mac na Ceàrdaich replicates the complex rhyme schemes, alliterations and four-line stanzas of classical Gaelic verse. He describes all the fauna that returns to Barra in the dusk to rest and take their sustenance from the island, contrasting it with the fate of the emigrants who will no longer do the same:

Ach an t-àl thug barrachd luaidh dhut,
A dhion t'uaill air chuan 's air tìr,
'S fheudar cùl thoirt ri 'n dualchas;
B' annsa cruas bhi 'n suain ad chill.

(*DMNC*, p. 86)

But the offspring who gave greater praise to you, / Who defended your dignity on sea and land, / Need to turn their backs on the land of their heritage; / 'Twould be a better hardship to sleep in your graveyard.

The climax of the poem showcases Mac na Ceàrdaich's ability to focus on crucial moments to encapsulate his themes, as the emigrants disappear over the horizon:

Beag fa dheòidh a chì mi uam thu
Dlùth mu'n cuairt ort shuain an oidhch'
Aon sealladh eile – sùil mo bhuairidh –
'S beannachd bhuan le d' shuaip a chaoidh!

(*DMNC*, p. 87)

Small at last I see you distantly / Close about you is night's slumber / One last glance – my vexation's sight – / A lasting blessing on your appearance for ever!

In a contrast with 'Fàilte gu Barraigh', the moment described encapsulates the grief and finality of the emigrants' experience, with the end-line emphasis on 'a chaoidh!' *('for ever!')* heightened by the exclamation as well as the dark tone given by the rhyme with 'oidhch'' (*'night'*).

Traditional Gaelic panygeric verse in both vernacular and classical Gaelic would frequently have a parting blessing for the subject, or their spouse, and Mac na Ceàrdaich utilises this in his own 'Beannachd'. The disappearance of the island into the night is followed by a verse in praise of the inheritance they take from Barra's 't' Aidmheil Naomh 's do chànain uasal' ('*Your sacred creed and noble language*') and then a dedication of the island to the Virgin Mary:

A Mhoire Mhìn bi dhuinn ad Mhàthair,
Sgiath do ghràidh biodh làidir linn;
O, leag do shùil air t' innis àraid,
Sìn do Làmh le bàidh 'san dìth.

(*DMNC*, p. 87)

Meek Mary be unto us a Mother, / May your shield of love be strong with us; / O, turn your eyes to your special isle, / Reach out your hand with tenderness in their loss.

The formality of this conclusion makes the understated shift in the emigrants' perspective all the more poignant at the end of each couplet. The prepositional pronouns 'linn' (*'with us'*), i.e. the emigrants, and "'san' (*'in their'*), i.e. the remaining Barra islanders, subtly encapsulate this break in the connection with their homeland, and the new perspective of the emigrants.

Religious and Celtic Revival imagery are frequently intertwined in Mac na Ceàrdaich's lyrical work, as is clear in 'A' Bheannachd Bharrach'. **'Ròs Aluinn'** (*'A Beautiful Rose'*) (*DMNC*, pp. 72–73) was one of three pieces by Mac na Ceàrdaich that appeared in the first edition of *An Ròsarnach* – the *Rose Garden* or *Rosary* – another Marr-funded periodical in 1917. Mac na Ceàrdaich appears to have chosen or been asked to write a poem along similar lines to the title of the publication. Its eleven verses typify Mac na Ceàrdaich's interests in symbolist and Celtic Revival imagery alongside Catholic iconography, whilst using a structure that refers to Classical Gaelic poetry. Focusing on the symbol of the rose, it's only in the second half of the poem that Mac na Ceàrdaich discusses the physical form of the rose, whilst even then it is in rather abstract terms.

The same year Mac na Ceàrdaich reviewed T. F. O'Rahilly's *Danta Gràdha*, an anthology of Classical Gaelic love poetry from Ireland and Scotland, and there are clear influences of these older formal pieces in the complicated rhyme scheme[1] and high register of much of the language. Mac na Ceàrdaich uses a traditional four-line stanza throughout and a circular ending that refers back to the initial verse.

O, m' annsachd ort, A Dhealbh na Maise;
'Aiteil chaoin de ghlòir na' Flathas;

---

1 For a brief introduction to Gaelic rhyme schemes, the introductions of W. J. Watson's *Bàrdachd Ghàidhlig*; McLeod and Bateman's *Duanaire na Sracaire*; or Bill Innes's introduction to *Aeòlus* can be consulted.

'Aisling naomh nan aing'la geala;
'Iomhaigh bheannaichte na h-Òighe!

(*DMNC*, p. 72)

O, my beloved, Beauty's Figure; / Tender glimpse of glory in paradise / Sacred dream of the white angels; / Blessed image of the Virgin!

The opening vocative 'O' and formal style clearly refer back to the classical Gaelic poets, whilst sharing Mac na Ceàrdaich's interest in the nature poems of the English Romantics. The poet builds up a litany of praise terms in the first half of the poem, on occasion using two to a line. These mix the Catholic and Celtic Revival imagery, such as the angels and virgin, with abstractions such as 'Maise' (*'Beauty'*) above.

The meditative repetitive nature of the poem allows Mac na Ceàrdaich to develop key imagery. The 'Aisling naomh nan aing'la geala' (*'sacred dream of the white angels'*) of the first stanza, transforms into ''S tusa 'm pong de cheol nan aingeal' (*'You're the note of angelic music'*) and then 'Tosgaire an gheallaidh néimhidh' (*'Messenger of the heavenly promise'*). This is echoed by the imagery of the penultimate stanza, dealing with the physical nature of the 'chlann na sgéithe' (*'sons of the wing'*) being a kenning for pollinators, as well as angels, with the poet wishing he could be counted amongst them drinking the flowers' sweetness:

Neò 'n e aon de chlann na sgéithe
'Gheibh do ghaol mar mhil do chléibhe?
O, ma 's e, – carson nach feudadh
Mise féin a bhi de'n àl sin?

(*DMNC*, p. 73)

> Or is it one of the wingèd children / Who gets your love like
> your bosom's sweetness? / O, if so – why could I not / myself
> be one of that brood.

The Celtic imagery used would be broadly familiar to his readers from Alexander Carmichael's *Carmina Gadelica*. As a city-based poet Mac na Ceàrdaich had an interesting relationship with the Revival specifically as someone who was from a community where much of the religious imagery and materials were collected by Carmichael. He was perhaps uniquely placed as a published creative writer during the Revival as somebody who was familiar with both Carmichael's renderings and who had been brought up in the the communities from which they had emerged. In this poem the epithets 'Mac na Gile' (lit. '*Son of Whiteness*', Carmichael translates as '*Son of the Moon*') and 'Mac na Speur' ('*Son of the Sky*') are likely taken from one of two Christmas gifting songs that were published in Volume I of *Carmina Gadelica*.[1] Mac na Ceàrdaich may well have been familiar with the oral original as one of Carmichael's informants for the songs was from neighbouring Mingulay.

The Tìr nan Òg imagery also featured prominently in the Celtic Revival, particularly due to the Irish writers and W. B. Yeats who first used it in *The Wanderings of Oisin*. Whilst it retains its role as the location of the afterlife in this poem, it also refers to a world of poetic truth and forms contrasted with the transient corrupt world of the present. The desire to drink the nectar of the rose, as in the stanza above, is thus enjoying

---

1 See both: 'Heire Bannag, Hoire Bannag', pp. 140–41 and 'Bannag nam Buadh', pp. 142–43, *Carmina Gadelica* (T. &. A. Constable, 1900), p. 1. For further discussion on these terms and translations see Ronald Black, 'God of the Moon, God of the Sun' in *West Highland Free Press*, 5 January 1996, accesssible online at: www.querndust.co.uk/PDFs/245DiaGile.pdf

the beatific vision that allows that world to be accessible. Yeats also used the rose symbol throughout his work, building on the esoteric tradition of European mysticism.

The poem remains a sophisticated and disciplined symbolist meditation that is innovative in its combination of abstract ideals, the heady accumulation of Revival epithets and the development of key images. At the same time it retains a connection with the wider Gaelic tradition by being a tightly structured panegyric. If it is not quite the 'Not Burns, Dunbar!' as MacDiarmid was to argue for in the years to come it is certainly a concerted engagement for a contemporary reader with the formal styles of poetry from earlier centuries. In the following decades Somhairle MacGill-eain who rated 'Ròs Aluinn' as 'very fine' in correspondence with Grieve, would also give a prominent place to the rose symbol including in poem 'LIV' of *Dàin do Eimhir*:

> Bu tu camhanaich air a' Chuilthionn
> 's latha suilbhir air a' Chlàraich,
> grian air a h-uilinn ann an òr-shruth
> agus ròs geal bristeadh fàire.
>
> Lainnir sheòl air linne ghrianaich,
> gorm a' chuain is iarmailt àr-bhuidh,
> an òg-mhaduinn 'na do chuailean
> 's 'na do ghruaidhean soilleir àlainn.
>
> Mo leug camhanaich is oidhche
> t' aodann is do choibhneas gràdhach
> ged tha bior glas an dòlais
> troimh chliabh m' òg-mhaidne sàthte.
>
> (Somhairle MacGill-eain,
> *Dàin do Eimhir* [MacLellan, 1943], p. 43)

You were dawn on the Cuilin / and benign day on the Clarach / the sun on his elbow in the golden stream / and the white rose that breaks the horizon. / / Glitter of sails on a sunlit firth / blue of the ocean and aureate sky, / the young morning in your head of hair / and in your clear lovely cheeks. / / My jewel of dawn and night / your face and dear kindness, / through the grey barb of misfortune is / thrust through the breast of my young morning.[1]

Mac na Ceàrdaich's interest in eternal truths, as seen in 'Ròs Aluinn', leads to a rejection of the materialist philosophy which he saw as being an extension of man's hubris. In **'An Duradan Duslaich'** (*'The Speck of Dust'*)[2] (*DMNC*, pp. 65–66) Mac na Ceàrdaich's address to a speck of dust, plays with the convention of lyrical praise of significant objects. He looks at the grain of dirt in turn as an electrical engineer, idealist and Catholic writer; talking about its physical properties; materialism as a philosophy and the mute humility he sees in the created world. He finds his repeated interests of scientific hubris, religious humility and poetic vision are encapsulated in his subject.

The highly rhetorical style suggests recitation rather than private contemplation, although the depth of the consideration of the subject matter would certainly permit the latter. Mac na Ceàrdaich uses the poetic vocative 'O' and the everyday vocative 'a' in commencing his poem before protesting his modesty as behoves tackling such a mighty subject:

---

1 Translation by MacGill-eain as published in *Nua-Bhàrdachd Ghàidhlig – Modern Gaelic Poetry* (Canongate, 1987), pp. 72–73.

2 Whilst the translation 'The Speck of Dust' captures the central meaning of Mac na Ceàrdaich's title, the alternatives of 'mote' and 'atom' are also relevant given the themes of the poem.

> O, thus' a neòini; thus' a ta cho faoin
> Fo chois nan daoi 's nan saoi an diugh 's an dé
> Gabh leisgeul bràthar théid ad' dhàil gu fòil
> Ga d' thogail sòluimte gu ruig a leus:
>
> (*DMNC*, p. 65)

> *O, you, nothing; you who are so trifling / Underfoot the wicked and wise today and yesterday / Excuse your brother gently coming to meet you / Lifting you solemnly to reach his gaze:*

This contrast between a high-flung poetic rhetoric and lowly subject matter reflects the dynamic in the poem of a disregarded bit of dirt being held up, solemnly, to lead a meditation on man's existence.

One of the recurring words in the poem is 'faoin'[1] – to Mac na Ceàrdaich the earth and geological time make clear the vaingloriousness of much of mankind's boasting of progress and achievement.

> Thig Eòlas pròiseil ann ad' chòir le stràic,
> Le gloine 's àsuinn dh' iarraidh dàn do chrè, –
> An leanabh beag a chaidh a bhreith an raoir
> Ag iarraidh 'ghreim a chur ma'n chruinne-ché.
>
> (*DMNC*, p. 66)

> *Proud knowledge comes into your presence with a clatter, / With glass and apparatus seeking your core's ken, – / The little babe that was born last night / Wanting to grasp the universe.*

---

[1] Variously translated by Edward Dwelly as '1 Vain, foolish. 2 Idle. 3 Unavailing. 4 Empty. 5 Light. 6 Lonely. 7 Trifling. 8** Useless.'

For Mac na Ceàrdaich there should be an awesome humility in respect of creation, but not a divinising of material as supreme arbiter of history. Mac na Ceàrdaich is not making an anti-scientific argument, rather he finds the reification of material facile given his professional awareness of humanity's ignorance of its nature:

> Mar 's diomhain sin, is diomhain sgil nan àl
> A thuigsinn fàth an neirt tha 'tàth do nì;
> A' chumhachd mhór ud a tha snaim a ghaineamh
> Co a dh' airmheas – seach a h-ainm – co i?
> (*DMNC*, p. 66)

Just as that is futile, as futile is the skill of that lot / In understanding the cause of the strength that binds you; / The great power that ties its grain / Who can compute – rather than name – what it is?

Mac na Ceàrdaich in essence undercuts the certainty of a crude materialist philosophy by highlighting man's ignorance of that self-same material. In terms of the specific elemental forces he refers to, it wasn't until the 1930s that the strong nuclear force which binds nuclei together would be discovered and calculated. Alongside his 1924 prose work, **'Litir Dhachaidh'** (*'A Letter Home'*) (*DMNC*, pp. 422–425), 'Duradan' is perhaps his most clear disagreement with the materialist philosophers and shows a clear scepticism or disillusionment with the idea of scientific progress. By using a Burnsian address to a humble object, Mac na Ceàrdaich is able to focus in on the materialist debates and scientific progress of his own day, whilst putting across his own reflections. As was clear in his anti-war essay **'Innis-na-Bréige'** (*DMNC*, pp. 351–59) there is an anger and disillusionment in Mac na Ceàrdaich's writing about the First World War. 'An Duradan

Duslaich' encapsulates this disillusionment at nineteenth-century technological progressivism which for all the rhetoric of progress left millions of his generation lost in the dirt of Flanders.

Also from 1917 **'Gairm Dusgaidh'** (*'Wake-Up Call'*) (*DMNC*, pp. 67–69) shares its rhetorical style with 'Duradan'. It is, however, a more overtly political poem, looking at the Gaelic community in a nationalist context. 'Gairm Dusgaidh' shares the short rhetorical clauses, direct address, alliterations and exclamations that distinguish these poems from his more lyrical works.

The poem functions as a brosnachadh (*incitement*), a genre which goes back to at least the Battle of Harlaw (1411) and the MacMhuirich hereditary poets to the Lords of the Isles. Mac na Ceàrdaich refers disapprovingly to Lachluinn MacMhuirich's incitement in 'Inbhe ar Bàrdachd' but in 'Gairm Dusgaidh' he shares the call to action and references to past glories found in the Brosnachadh Catha (*Incitement to Battle*) – for both Mac na Ceàrdaich and MacMhuirich the key is 'cuimhneachaibh' (*'remember'*).

Mac na Ceàrdaich uses revival imagery found elsewhere in his poetry but the style is very different:

> Dùisg a Ghàidheil! Dùisg á sin o d' shuain!
> Feuch 'san ear! Seall a' ghrian á cuan
> Ag éirigh fòs 'na glòir, 'na h-òige nuadh!
> Tha 'n saoghal sean, ged tha, tha earrach uain'
> A' dearbhadh Aois mar sgleò.
>
> (*DMNC*, p. 67)

Awaken, Gaels! Awaken there from your slumber! / Behold the East! See the sun from sea / Rising yet in glory, in new youth! / The world's old, but still, the green spring / Proves Age a shadow.

Mac na Ceàrdaich is confidently using the imagery of the Celtic Revival to address Scotland's Gaels, which is notable in its post-Easter Rising context. The verdant, primaveral imagery and sun rising over the horizon were all popular images of the Revival. The initial emphasis on 'Ag éirigh' in the third line following the enjambement showcases this complex verbal noun variously translated by Dwelly as: *rising, mounting, rebellion, ascension, mutiny, prospering.*

Overall, and despite the idyllic opening, the poem is very dark in tone. Mac na Ceàrdaich compares the Gaels and their predicament as a minoritised culture working to advance the British Empire, and by extension their own irrelevance, to the 'chuilein coin air fead do fhear na spréidh' (*DMNC*, p. 67) ('*the pup under the drover's whistle*'). The intergenerational impact of the breakdown of community language transmission is also a prime concern 'ghlaisean maol a' suidh air ubh na cuaich' / 'S a' togail isean nach leis féin – mo thruaigh'!' (*DMNC*, p. 67) ('*the swallow sat on the cuckoo's nest / And raising a chick that's not its own – my ruin!*'). He develops this using the changeling imagery of Gaelic legend: "'S am bodach glas an riochd do leinibh féin / A thréig thu ann ad' shuain' (*DMNC*, p. 67) ('*And the old grey man in your child's guise / Whom you'd abandoned in your slumber*'). Rather than secure the future of their own culture via the next generation, Mac na Ceàrdaich believes the Gaels' desire for material advancement and imperial loyalty has curbed their vision and will to develop and maintain their own culture. The next generation is in turn pictured as 'a' bùrach làraichean, is anns na tuill / A' sireadh guth a dh' eug!' (*DMNC*, p. 68) ('*poking about in graves, and in the holes / seeking a voice that's died!*').

Mac na Ceàrdaich shares with MacDiarmid and T. S. Eliot the concerns that industrial societies had a homogenising effect. These anxieties were exacerbated by the First World War and perhaps were felt most accutely in minoritised cultures and languages; where state hostility and indifference meant the homogenisation would pose an existential threat. However, Mac na Ceàrdaich's criticism is directed inward to his own community for aping another culture: 'Bheil bith seach bith ag aoradh chàch a chéil'?' (*DMNC*, p. 69) ('*Does one being or another idolise each other?*'). In his analysis, Gaels maintain agency over their own fate and if they cease to exist it will have been a suicide:

> 'S e 'bhreith bheir Fìrinn agus Ceartas treun
> 'Thug an Gàidheal 'n uthachd so dha féin,
> Na coiricheam a nàmh!'
>
> (*DMNC*, p. 68)
>
> *The judgement Truth and mighty Justice shall give is / 'The Gael did this suicide to himself, / I won't blame his foes!'*

As a writer in a minority culture whose existence requires resistance to homogenisation on the majority culture's terms Mac na Ceàrdaich overtly states his anxiety that his community will end up undistinguished in the tide of humanity. It's worth quoting the section in full:

> Tha mi fo iomagain is le eagal làn
> Gu'n téid thu leis an t-slochd.
> Do'n t-slochd 's nach aithnichear thu am measg na spràig
> A dh'fhàg an tiùrr an sin 'na aona chàrn,
> 'S co dhiu b'ann odhar, dubh, no geal, no ruadh
> Nach inns do theanga mar a toirear tuairms
> Bho dhealbh 's o chruas do chnàmh.
> Seadh, tuairmse dhall, – A! Mhic, an tig an uair,
> An tig an là 'san sloinnear t'àl air thuairms?
>
> (*DMNC*, pp. 67–68)

> *I am worried and of fear full / That you'll go with the pit. / Into the pit where you are not recognised amidst the spray / That the tide left there in one heap, / And regardless of whether sallow, black, or white, or red / Your tongue won't reveal like taking a guess / From appearance and strength of bone. / Aye, a blind guess, – O! Son, will the hour come, / Will the day come when your children are named by guess?*

Referring to skin colour and the faux-science of bone densities is jarring for a contemporary reader, even in the context of Mac na Ceàrdaich's view that they are bogus science and 'tuairmse dall' (*'blind guesswork'*). As is clear both within the poem and elsewhere in his work, Mac na Ceàrdaich's concern is arguing for equality for Gaels rather than a chauvinistic superiority, a view he dismantles on a number of occasions. His criticism of these approaches is itself a reminder of how prevalent they were in imperial Britain, however.

Thereafter, the despair and dark imagery gives way to a tone more like the opening lines, with revival imagery of the Gaels and Tir nan Òg emerging from the Twilight:

> O mhullach bheann, thar ghleann is shrath is chuan
> Mo ghlaodh so sgaoileam air na gaothan luath',
> 'S gu'n cluinn an craoitear e 's an t-iasgair thall,
> 'S gach neach tha dùthchasach do thìr nam beann.
> 'S gu'n gabh sinn suim a dheanamh tùirn mar 's còir
> An déis dhuinn dùsgadh as an dùsal mhór;
> 'S gu'n téid sinn comhla, sean is òg 's gu léir
> Gu àird nan sliabh 'chur fàilte air a' Ghréin;
> Air toiseach aimsir nuadh.
> Oir tha mo shùil a' dearcadh dàn nan Dùl,
> Is chi mi solus dealrach air an cùl;

Solus ùror o bheil Gaol a' snàmh,
Maise 's Aoibhneas agus Sonas làn,
Is uidh air n-uidh tha 'n dealbh a' lìonadh fòs
Gu'n tog mi soilleir iargail Tìr-nan-Òg.

(*DMNC*, p. 69)

From mountain top, over glen and strath and sea / My cry I spread on the swift winds / That yonder crofter and fisherman may hear, / And each person belonging to the highlands. / That we will take heed to do a turn as we should / After we awaken from the great slumber; / And we'll go together, old and young and all / To the muir's top to welcome the Sun; / At the beginning of a new age. / For my eyes see the fate of All Things, / And I see a bright light behind them; / A new light from whence Love swims / Beauty and Joy and Happiness complete, / And bit by bit the picture fills yet / Till I clearly see Tìr nan Òg's evening twilight.

The Twilight and graveyard imagery also make a prominent appearance in his 1930 poem **'Slighe nan Seann Seun'** (*'The Way of the Old Charms'*) (*DMNC*, p. 96). This is Mac na Ceàrdaich's language at its most densely lyrical,[1] with the poet using alliteration and internal rhyme throughout which further emphasises the cultural richness that is his theme.

The poet initially describes the warm light and peaceful atmosphere overlooking the sea on a quiet island evening. However, the peacefulness serves to draw attention to an absence which the poet goes on to relay – former days and a community that inexorably continues to decline. This is

---

1 Such that Hugh MacDiarmid, most likely echoing his Gaelic translator Somhairle MacGill-eain, highlights the difficulties in translating it, a view seconded by Ronald Black and the present author. Stanzas from the poem first appear in the 1927 prose piece 'Dealachadh nan Rathad' (*DMNC*, pp. 426–31)

confirmed in the final stanza where he describes a graveyard by the shore:

> Cha neonach cill mo shluaigh an cois nan cuan bhi balbh,
> Chan ioghnadh uchd nan tuam bhi 'n tòic le luach na dh'fhalbh,
> O, shaoghail, is truagh nach tìll aon uair a shearg,
> 'S nach tàrr mo dheòin, ge buan, aon fhios á suain nam marbh!
> (*DMNC*, p. 96)

Not strange that my people's kirkyard by the sea is silent, / No wonder the tombs' breasts are swollen with the worth that's gone, / O, world, it's a pity that not one hour that's faded will return, / And that my will, though enduring, won't draw one word from the dead's slumber!

Unlike 'Gairm-Dusgaidh' there is no positive ending. He is most likely describing St Brendan's graveyard, where he was subsequently interred, which sits out by the Atlantic on the West Coast of Barra. Mac na Ceàrdaich's descriptions project his emotional state outwards. The natural phenomena are personified 'Sona gnùis nan cuan' ('*Happy the sea's aspect*') and 'aigne suaimhneach ghaoth' ('*the wind's peaceful spirit*'). This initial happiness, however, is in recalling days that have since departed 'am bruadair uair a dh'aom' ('*in a dream of a time that's waned*'). The ending of the poem in the graveyard captures the paradoxical richness of being alone in a place where generations of your forebears were buried.

There is an appropriateness to the themes of Mac na Ceàrdaich's final poem. The decline of his community and culture, as well as the passing of the Celtic Revival aesthetic captured in its title, are all evident. However, it also points a way forward in the way it grants high esteem and status to his language and culture. The dense language and lyrical focus is innovative, prefiguring Somhairle MacGill-eain's 'Hallaig' and other poems of the next generation that speak with lyrical clarity of absence in a landscape.

It would be remiss not to consider the role of community in Mac na Ceàrdaich's work, given the prominence of songs for performance and the anxiety about the deterioration of Gaelic communities seen throughout his work. His songs cover many of the themes that emerge in popular poetry of the period including reportage and satire. **'Oran do na Fasain'** (*'A Song to the Fashions'*) (*DMNC*, pp. 99–100) portrays the extravagence of Edwardian upper-class women's fashion to a Barra audience. Whilst Morningside's ladies would be known for the apocryphal 'fur coat and no knickers', what's most striking about Mac na Ceàrdaich's poem is the use of traditional oral techniques such as rhythm and onomatopoiea to suit his subject. Mac na Ceàrdaich uses adjectives and word-order to build up the strangeness of all the various accessories he's describing and create an aural image of the lady's bustles following behind them:

> Air mullach na h-uiread bidh cunnart còt-uachdair
> 'Chomhdaicheas uil' iad gu bunaibh an cluasan,
> Shaoileadh gach duine a chluinneadh an gluasad
> Gun robh am Fuathas tighinn air a thòir.
>
> (DMNC, p. 100)

On top of all that there's a risk of an overcoat / That covers them all to base of their ears / Each person who heard them in motion would think / that the Devil was chasing after him.

Mac na Ceàrdaich tells his audience that it is difficult for him even to try and describe the exotic clothing, and accompanying names for each item:

> An còmhdach 's an caisbheart chan aithne dhomh trian dheth
> Ainmean annasach, cam-fhaclach, lìonmhor;
> 'S air cho ro-mhath is gun taghainn mo bhriathran
> Gheibhinn droch dhìol gan cur air an dòigh.
> (DMNC, p. 99)

Their covering and their footwear I don't recognise a third of it / Exotic names, crooked-worded, and plenty of them; / No matter how well I choose my words / I'll get a poor reward putting them in order.

Whilst a man commenting on a woman's appearance is not likely to meet with approval today, the context of satirising the upper-classes for a working-class audience as well as inverting the power dynamics between a minority and majority culture means that the poem should not be discounted immediately on that basis. The social reportage role of this poetry is mentioned early in the poem:

> Bhon tha mi car tamaill am Baile na Smùide,
> Faicinn gach annais is car thig air cùisean
> Bheir mi mo bharail gun mhearachd, gun lùb
> Gur mór a' chùis-bhùirsd tha 'n cuideachd nan sròl.
> (DMNC, p. 99)

As I'm a while in the Smokey City, / Seeing each novelty and fashion that fleets by / I will give my opinion without mistake or guile / What a great laughing stock are those wrapped up in silks.

The song can be contrasted with **'Cailleachan an t-Snaoisean'** (*'The Old Women of Snuff'*) (*DMNC*, pp. 107–08) where Mac na Ceàrdaich describes the snuff taking, drinking and singing in good humour before sending his regards to the women. Community poetry had a role in both strengthening the cohesion of the group through humour and good-natured satire and Mac na Ceàrdaich does that successfully.

7. LÀ NAN SEACHD SION (1915–16) (*THE DAY OF THE SEVEN ELEMENTS*)

At just under eight hundred lines Mac na Ceàrdaich's longest poetic work is an epic poem describing a storm hitting a Hebridean island. It narrates the imperilment of a local fishing boat and the community ashore. This is a topic with an important precedent in the Gaelic literary tradition. Mac na Ceàrdaich, however, imbues it with his own concerns of pacificism, idealism and Marian theology all of which bring new concerns to the fore. The poem has seven sections and appeared in 1915–16 in editions of *Guth na Bliadhna*. Mac na Ceàrdaich was living and working in London at this time, as the full horrors of the First World War became more and more apparent.

Whilst the Ship of State as an image in European literature was used at least as early as ancient Greece, in vernacular Scottish Gaelic literature the theme of an epic sea voyage was most famously used by Alasdair Mac Mhaighstir Alasdair (*Alexander MacDonald*) in his poem *Birlinn Clann Raghnaill*. At over five hundred lines, the poem describes how the Chief of Clanranald and his crew are caught in a storm en-route to Ireland. This poem was written in the post-Culloden Gàidhealtachd, specifically in the Clanranald communities that saw some of the worst reprisals from the Hanovarian government forces. As a soldier who fought at Prestonpans and Culloden, and whose house was burned down by the redcoats, Mac Mhaighstir Alasdair's imagery of sulphurous smoke and roaring thunder has been interpreted as directly reflecting the canonade at Culloden. Regardless of whether there was a direct historical basis for the imagery he uses, he set an important precedent of a ship's voyage through a storm being an allegory of a crisis that Mac na Ceàrdaich reinvigorated in 1915–16 and which was later utilised by Dòmhnall Ruadh Phàislig (*Donald MacIntyre*) in 1938 in his poem 'Aeòlus agus am Balg' ('*Aeòlus and the Bellows*') to satirise the three Fascist dictators.

It would be wrong to think of this poem (or indeed any poem) as solely a Gaelic production, shaped by the Gaelic literary tradition in isolation. The opening image of an aged fisherman, and indeed the formal structure of seven sections initially with four-line stanzas and an *abab* rhyme scheme owe more to the example of nineteenth-century English poet Samuel Taylor Coleridge's 'The Rime of the Ancient Mariner' than to Mac Mhaighstir Alasdair. Mac na Ceàrdaich starts with:

> Leugh treabhaich aosmhor nan tonn
> Clar-amais màirneul nan sion;
> Bu daingeann a chreideamh 'na chom,
> Gun teagamh 's gun fhonn bha 'bhriathar.
>
> (*DMNC*, p. 42)

> *The aged ploughman of waves read / The sky's navigating index; / Secure was the belief in his heart, / Without doubt, without flourish, his words.*

The poet's interest in signs and meaning is clear from the language of these first sections. The physical world is portrayed as a book that can be 'read' by those with sufficient knowledge and certainty. These images are repeated throughout the opening: 'comharradh soilleir sin riamh / Nach tainig gun fhior 'na chois' (*DMNC*, p. 42) ('*that clear mark that never / Came without truth in its wake*') and 'Chaidh sanas gu aire gach eòin' (*DMNC*, p. 43) ('*A sign went to the attention of each bird'*) in a similar vein. This continues into the following sections with:

> Oir 's soileir bha d'a shealladh-san
> Droch mhanadh air an speur:
> 'S an cuan cha d' chùm am falach air
> a shanas dùth neo-mhearachdach;
>
> (*DMNC*, p. 45)

For clear to his sight were the / Ill omens on the heavens: / And the sea did not hide from him / Its unmistakable proper warning;

This interest in interpreting meaning spotlights a key figure who appears elsewhere in his work: the master mariner. Their forecasting and navigation skills, that look for order in a chaotic world of nature, act as an extended metaphor for the poet's ability to name truths more readily than his contemporaries. This idealistic and prophetic role assigned to poetry is outlined in more detail in 'Inbhe ar Bàrdachd' (*DMNC*, pp. 332–41) and revisited in the 1921 short story 'Lughain Lir' (*DMNC*, pp. 399–421). Mac na Ceàrdaich inherits from Coleridge a sense of non-changing ideals with the poets being able to interpret the eternal signs, or Forms in a Platonic sense, that lie behind everyday experience.

In practical terms, it is also the mariner who senses the shift in the weather and in sections I and III ensures the vessel's survival. He has a prophetic duty to truth that is reflected in 'gun teagamh 's gun fhonn' (*DMNC*, p. 42) (*'without doubt, without flourish'*) in the opening lines, or the lack of 'briot no briathrachais' (*DMNC*, p. 46) (*'tattle or verbosity'*) in III. In a positive and active sense it is the mariner who says the blessing whilst pouring the holy water into the sea preventing the boat being swamped at the poem's midpoint and giving them some respite from the storm. For Mac na Ceàrdaich, it is those who can see order in the disordered world who can best navigate it should they have sufficient certainty, and it is their responsibility to share these truths transparently with others.

Religious Narrative

This interest in finding meaning in a disordered world takes on an explicitly religious aspect. As in 'Fearann a Shinnsir' and 'Lughain Lir', Catholic faith is fundamental to the key moments in the poem's narrative. Mac na Ceàrdaich structures the poem's midpoint and climax on two religious images. The first is the fishermen praying in their boat 'An t-Ealasaid' (*'The Elizabeth'*) in III:

> Mar neach le urras Fhlathanais
> Nach toireadh muir a bheatha dheth
> Rinn stiùramaich an achanaich
> Le creidimh daingeann treun,
> Sin thionndaidh e gu h-abalta
> Ri iùnrais a' Chuain Phabaich ud
> Is chrath e'n craos an amh-bhoinne
> An ainm an Trianaid Dhé.
>
> (*DMNC*, p. 48)

Like one with heaven's assurance / The sea would not take his life from him / The helmsman made the supplication / With a secure, mighty faith, / Then he turned readily / To that Pabbay Sea's tempest / And he shook the pure droplets into the gullet / In the name of the Triune God.

The extract shows the mariner taking on a religious role, with his religious faith reflecting his navigational certainties elsewhere in these sections. The *aaab* rhyme scheme follows the assonantal rhyme rules in Scottish Gaelic and runs throughout this section. It is a direct echo of 'Birlinn Clann Raghnaill' and the 'iorram' metre most typical of rowing songs in Scottish Gaelic. This has an irregular number of short lines with an *a*-ending which concludes by a longer line with a *b*-ending. The use of 'An t-Ealasaid' as the name of the vessel stems directly from the practice in the southern Outer Hebrides of giving Marian names to fishing vessels. As the Virgin Mary's relation and mother of John the Baptist, who is the culmination of the prophets in the Catholic tradition, it strengthens the connection between the master mariner and the prophetic poet.

The other primary turning point of the poem is the narrative climax, where an unnamed mother prays to a Christian God who orders the cessation of the storm. This further Marian image concludes VI:

> Lùb màthair leanabh a glùin
> Is chuir i glan-ùrnuigh suas;
> Ag iarraidh cobhair air Dia
> 'S ag achanaich siochaint luath.
> Mar thora a' tolladh troimh chruaidh
> Chaidh a guidhe troimh ghruaim nan sion,
> Is ràinig Athair nam Beò
> Air Cathair na Trocair Shior.
> Fhuair iobairt bheannaicht' a crìdh
> Làn airidh 'o Thì nan dùl
> Is dh'òrdaich Esan fa-dheòigh
> Grad-fhosadh na comhraig dhùir.
>
> (*DMNC*, p. 58)

A babe's mother bent her knee / And sent a pure prayer upwards / Asking God for aid / And entreating a quick peace. / Like an auger drilling through steel / Her prayer went through the element's gloom / And reached the Father of the Living / On the Throne of Eternal Mercy. / Her heart's blessèd sacrifice / Received full due from the Lord of All / And he ordered at long last / A cessation to the obstinate combat.

The extended quote shows the narrative impact of this act by an anonymous woman at the poem's climax. It also demonstrates the mixture of religious and wartime imagery that are two overlapping themes of the poem. There is a freely bestowed grace that one small act of entreating is granted, which undercuts the obvious power of the storm that has been demonstrated at length up until this penultimate section. This structural contrast of hundreds of lines of exposition being undone by the prayer of one woman is reflective of Marian Christian theology, in that it represents the petitionary power of the humble leading to the response of the omnipotent.

The interest in the humblest of characters is also shown in Mac na Ceàrdaich's ecological concerns. These reflected the exaltation of the humble as a theme in Christian literature, whether they be beggars, shepherds or fisherman. More specifically he also utilised the medieval tradition of a world in which the creator has left a physical impression. Traditions such as robins having red breasts due to blood from Calvary were recorded in the twentieth-century Highlands by fieldworkers from the School of Scottish Studies. Using this idea of nature as a book that can be interpreted in light of the Gospel allows Mac na Ceàrdaich to reinforce the connections between interpretating the natural world, and a Christian creator God putting order on it. This interest in the state of Creation coupled with a belief in a personal God is clear immediately prior to the mother's petition:

Is c' àite bheil caoirich is féidh
'S gach beathach 'tha 'cheum air sliabh?

Gun fhasgadh, leaba no blàths
Gun fhuras, gun tàmh, gun bhiadh,
Gun seòl, gun chothrom, gun sgeum
Air teicheadh 'o bheud nan sion, –
Aig Dia 'tha fios air an càs,
'S do 'n urrainn 's le 'n aill an dion.

(*DMNC*, p. 58)

And where are the sheep and deer / And each animal who walks the moor? / No shelter, bed or warmth / No peace, no rest, no food, / No method, no chance, no scheme / Of fleeing the peril of the elements, – / God only knows their plight, / Who can and wishes to defend them.

The challenge that the question and repetition above poses, which would have reverberated in the summer of 1916, is how could a personal God who cares for creation tolerate such levels of destruction and loss of life? Indeed, Mac na Ceàrdaich's use of imagery ensures that the wartime context is directly tied to the storm's impact.

Martial Imagery

The disorder of the natural world is clear throughout the poem and it's in this imagery of disorder that the First World War's impact is most noticeable. From IV onwards, the storm is portrayed in increasingly martial terms. We have seen the mixture of religious and martial imagery at the poem's climax, where the orders of the omnipotent Creator are couched in terms of a peace treaty. But Mac na Ceàrdaich builds up to this point with V and VI featuring a number of bellicose images. This extract from the start of V uses performative language that reminds us that poetry was still being recited in the taigh-chèilidh with Mac na Ceàrdaich using the plural imperative:

Eisdibh – siod guth àrd nam mòr-chuan!
Eisdibh ri cath-ghairm nan sion!
Eug-cheòl ann am chluais an còmhnuidh;
Manadh dóruinn, creiche 's diol;
Manadh càis nam mac 's nan leannan;
Call nam fear 's nan athar gaoil;
Sanas cruaidh a' bhròin 's an leanduibh;
Màthair 's leanabh creacht' de'n aon.

(*DMNC*, pp. 51–52)

Listen – that's the great sea's high voice! / Listen to the elements' battle cry! / Death-music in my ears always; Omen of hardship, pillage and ruin; / Omen of sons' and lovers' predicaments; / The loss of men and beloved fathers; / The hard sign of sadness and melancholy; / Mother and child robbed of their loved one.

This focus on loss of menfolk applies equally to the great storms as it does to the World War. Mac na Ceàrdaich uses repetition, alliteration, anaphora and parallelisms for both onomatopoeic and thematic reasons, as he draws attention to the repetitive nature of the storm and the repeated losses being relayed to a wartime community. The interaction of storm and sea is cast as an old battle between the elements especially 'àrdan na mara' (*DMNC*, p. 52) ('*the sea's pride*') with further personification of the wind and rocks strengthening the wartime parallels. Specific vocabulary choice, 'armailt [...] ag iathadh' (*DMNC*, p. 52) ('*army assembling*') and 'feachd an uamhais' (*DMNC*, p. 53) ('*terror's host*') continue to be used in the extended elemental battle in V. In VI, where Mac na Ceàrdaich returns to the storm's impact ashore, he develops further obvious wartime images such as the cold blast hitting a gable-end is 'am peilear 'o ghualainn bheann' ('*bullet from a hill's shoulder*') and the simile 'mar mhothar cànain a bhrùchd / a bhrùthadh air ùrlar ghleann' (*DMNC*, p. 55) ('*like the roar of a cannon erupting / pounding the valley floor*').

Conclusion

As the interplay of religious imagery and martial terminology shows, Mac na Ceàrdaich's poem presents a rich array of allegorical considerations for readers. A more literal reading of the poem is as a historical narrative formed by his own experiences as a herring fisherman, from a family of fishermen. This has the advantage of bringing out the rich social history in the poem – the conditions in Castlebay are captured by the highly specific vocabularly referring to rising damp in black houses, or the rain water turning black as it descends through a foolish man's poorly maintained thatched roof. Mac na Ceàrdaich also uses the terminology he was familiar with from his family's fishing background: 'gormanachd éisg' (*DMNC*, p. 46), the act of removing fish from the hooks on a long-line.

Both a religious and contemporaneous allegorical reading of the poem are served by Mac na Ceàrdaich's compositional allegory – the sea and storm are at war and nature is disordered. This is made more explicit still in the imagery. Mac na Ceàrdaich's 1918 anti-war essay 'Innis-na-Brèige' (*DMNC*, pp. 351–59) would make it clear that he considered it morally repugnant, but even in 1914's *Crois-Tara!* there is a clear sceptism about military adventurism.

Conflict is a theme throughout. The eponymous elements are personified, such as the sea, 'Thréig a ciall i 's chaill i 'dòigh' (*DMNC*, p. 52) ('*[the sea's] sense left her and she lost her way*'). Moreover, there has been a relational breakdown between these elements: 'Oir chaidh gach cumhachd thar a chéile, / 'S throid gu reubalach ma 'n neart' (*DMNC*, p. 53)

('*As each power strove above the rest / Fighting rebelliously about their strength*'). This complete breakdown of right order is encapsulated in a simile that parallels Milton's *Paradise Lost* where angels throw the hills on the fallen angels. Mac na Ceàrdaich describes the rain clouds:

> Mar mhìle beinn aibheiseach chòrr
> A flathas a' toirleum luath
> Tigh'n bronnaich air tharraich troimh 'n fhàs
> 'S a' spraidheadh air clàir de'n chruaidh.
>
> (*DMNC*, p. 56)

> *Like a thousand vast hills more / From paradise leaping fast / Bellies swelling in girth, growing, / Then exploding on a rocky plain.*

The poem's conclusion, after order is restored by divine intervention, shows the men and women welcoming the 'Ealasaid' back to Castlebay, and then giving thanks. This takes us full circle back to Alasdair Mac Mhaighstir Alasdair, where the sailors arrive in Carrickfergus and do the same. Mac Mhaighstir Alasdair had been recognised as minimising the poetic focus on Clanranald himself by focusing on the crew, moving from a metonymical and monarchical courtly vision onto a more meritocractic focus on individual crew members. In turn Mac na Ceàrdaich's characters are anonymous. The mariner and the young mother ashore are imbued with an archetypal importance by this anonymity. And once order is finally restored in the world, these characters are all united at the conclusion of this twentieth-century epic.

8. CONCLUSION

This short introduction has outlined some of the ways Dòmhnall Mac na Ceàrdaich worked to reinvigorate Gaelic writing across multiple genres. In some cases he innovated from scratch, bringing in entirely new ideas and forms. He was proud to write in a minoritised language, and his writing remains a treasure trove for Scottish Gaelic communities, especially his home community of Barra.

Aside from the pleasure and stimulation that comes from engagement with his work, Mac na Ceàrdaich's writing sheds light on issues such as the Celtic Revival in Scotland, and how the Gaelic community engaged with this movement. He is also an important modern Scottish Catholic writer, whose work engages with themes shared with other writers in that tradition. The networks in which he operated whether in Edinburgh's Celtic Revival circles or Ruaraidh Erskine of Marr's political radicals could also be explored further.[1] This would also include his association with, and impact on, Christopher Murray Grieve and the advent of Hugh MacDiarmid and his Scottish Renaissance movement. Of course, there remains the possibility that correspondence from *DMNC*, Dòmhnall Mac na Ceàrdaich or Donald Sinclair will shed further light on these topics.

One of the aspects of his writing that has not been highlighted in this guide is his sense of humour – particularly in his comedies and songs – or his writing of two plays for children and its relationship to other Scottish children's literature or Revival drama.

Mac na Ceàrdaich's life was remarkable – from a Castlebay classroom to designing world-leading technology, a political

---

[1] Project ERSKINE, led by Dr Petra Poncarová at the University of Glasgow, is now exploring these networks.

activist and significant Scottish writer. His death at forty-six left a literary legacy that was not particularly well-recognised by academia for a number of decades. However, his work remains a shining example of the breadth and quality of creative work that was being written in Scottish Gaelic in the early twentieth century. Writing in 1974, Ruaraidh MacThòmais (*Derick Thomson*) stated that Sinclair's poetry's importance 'remains to be assessed in detail'. With the publication of Storey's collected edition of his works, this assessment can now continue apace.

9. SELECT BIBLIOGRAPHY

Storey, Lisa (ed.), *D.M.N.C.: Sgrìobhaidhean Dhòmhnaill Mhic na Ceàrdaich* (Clàr, 2014)

Black, Ronald (ed.), *An Tuil: Anthology of 20th Century Scottish Gaelic Verse* (Polygon, 1999)

Black, Ronald, 'Gaelic Prose' in *Scottish Literature and World War I*, ed. by David A. Rennie (Edinburgh University Press, 2022), pp. 122–42

—'Gaelic Verse' in *Scottish Literature and World War I*, pp. 100–121

—'God of the Moon, God of the Sun', *West Highland Free Press*, 5 January 1996, online at www.querndust.co.uk/PDFs/245DiaGile.pdf

Carmichael, Alexander (ed.), *Carmina Gadelica* (T. & A. Constable, 1900)

Innes, Bill, 'Introduction' in Donald MacIntyre, *Aeòlus!* (Grace Note, 2008), pp. xi–xxiii

MacAulay, Donald, *Nua-Bhàrdachd Ghàidhlig – Modern Scottish Gaelic Poems: A Bilingual Anthology* (Canongate, 1987)

MacCurdy, Edward, 'The Plays of Donald Sinclair', *Transactions of the Gaelic Society of Inverness*, 41 (1953), pp. 68–92

MacDiarmid, Hugh, 'Donald Sinclair' in *At the Sign of the Thistle* (Stanley Nott, 1934), pp. 80–88

—'English Ascendancy in British Literature', in *At the Sign of the Thistle*, pp. 11–32

—(ed.), *A Golden Treasury of Scottish Poetry* (Macmillan, 1940)

Mac Gill-eain, Somhairle, *Ris a' Bhruthaich: The Criticism and Prose Writings of Sorley MacLean*, ed. by William Gillies (Acair, 1985)

Mac Leòid, Aonghas, 'An Dàn Fada Gàidhealach: Sgrùdadh Ioma-Chuspaireil air Corpas air Dìochuimhne' (unpublished doctoral thesis, University of Glasgow, 2014)

—'Innis-na-Fìrinne: Dòmhnall Mac-na-Ceàrdaich agus a Obair Fhoillsichte' (unpublished masters dissertation, University of Glasgow, 2012)

—'The Historical Plays of Donald Sinclair', *International Journal of Scottish Theatre and Screen*, 9 (2016), pp. 24–38

—'Forgetting Donald Sinclair 1885–1932: the Passage Between Celtic Revival and Scottish Renaissance', *Scottish Language*, 37 (2018), pp. 55–72

Macleod, Donald, *Gloomy Memories* (Archibald Sinclair, 1892)

MacLeod, Donald John, 'Twentieth Century Gaelic Literature: a description, comprising critical study and a comprehensive bibliography' (unpublished doctoral thesis, University of Glasgow, 1969)

Macleod, Michelle (ed.), *Dràma na Gàidhlig: Ceud Bliadhna air an Àrd-Ùrlar* (Association for Scottish Literary Studies, 2021)

Macleod, Michelle and Moray Watson, 'In the Shadow of the Bard: The Gaelic Short Story, Novel and Drama since the early Twentieth Century', in *The Edinburgh History of Scottish Literature: Modern Transformation: New Identities*, ed. by Ian Brown, Thomas Clancy, Susan Manning and Murray Pittock (Edinburgh University Press, 2007), pp. 273–82

McLeod, Wilson, *Gaelic in Scotland: Policies, Movements, Ideologies* (Edinburgh University Press, 2020)

McLeod, Wilson and Meg Bateman (eds), *Duanaire na Sracaire: Songbook of the Pillagers Anthology of Scotland's Gaelic Verse to 1600* (Birlinn, 2007)

NicIain, Anna, 'Bàird a' Bhaile Againn', *Gairm*, 7 (1954), pp. 221–25

Ross, Susan, 'Identity in Scottish Gaelic Drama 1900–1949', *International Journal of Scottish Theatre and Screen*, 9 (2016), pp. 39–60

Shaw, Michael, *The Fin-de-Siècle Scottish Revival: Romance, Decadence and Celtic Identity*, Edinburgh Critical Studies in Victorian Culture (Edinburgh University Press, 2019)

Storey, Lisa, *Bhatarsaigh agus na Raiders* (Clò Phabaigh, 2023)

—*Muinntir Mhiughalaigh* (Clàr, 2007)

Thomson, Derick, *An Introduction to Gaelic Poetry* (Victor Gollancz, 1974)

Watson, Moray, *An Introduction to Gaelic Fiction* (Edinburgh University Press, 2011)

Watson, William J. (ed.), *Bàrdachd Ghàidhlig: specimens of Gaelic Poetry 1550–1900* (An Comunn Gàidhealach, 1932)

APPENDIX – POETRY TEXTS AND TRANSLATIONS

Faoileag an Droch-Chladaich (1913)

Iasgair:

'A Chreutair ghràdhaich gu dé'n stàth dhuit
A bhi 'n gnàth mu'n chòrsa so,
Far nach tàrr thu nì gu d' àillinn
'S tu gach là 'na d' ònaran.
Nach mór bu làn-doigheil do chàradh
A bhi tàmh 's na h-òbannan,
Far 'eil fàrdach sheasgair bhlàth dhuit
'S biadh 's an tràigh gun sòradh ort?

Innis dhomh, oir dh'fhairtlich orm,
Dé 'tha thu 'lorg a bhuannachd as,
'S nach fhaic mo shùil ach cladach borb
A' fùideach' colg nan stuaghannan.
An fhiosrach leat gu'n tug an dorgh
Bho'n aigeal ghorm na bhuaireadh thu,
'S an ealtainn uile 'n siod le toirm
A' solar soirbh an cnuasachd dheth?'

Faoileag:

'Ar leam, 'ill' òig, gur plaoisg do ghlòir
Is nach eil eòlas nàduir leat,
'S ged 's mór do chòir-s' air aithne chòrr,
Nach eil do chomhairl' ro thàbhachdach.
Ged tha mo bhòrd-sa lom de lòn
'An sùilean sòghail àrd-bhithean;

Tha mise, fòs, gun dìth gun bhròn
Is m' inntinn stòld' is sàthaichte.

Gu dé mhiannaichinn no 'dh' iarrainn
Bho nach ciocair tràilleil mi?
Ma tha mi riaraichte 's gun dìorras,
Nach eil tiodhlaic 's àirde leam?
Ma tha mo bhiadh is m' àite-dion
Gun uireas fìor d'a m'chàileachdan,
Tha suim mo thiarma 'cheart cho fiachar
Is ged b' eun le bànrigh'n mi.

Creid mi, 'ille! cha'n e dòigh
No socair-shògh gu'n sàthaich thu.
Creid mi! cha'n e eadhoin còir
Air Roinn na h-Eorpa 'bhàrr air sin.
Ach 's e bheir sonas dhuit a' d' bheò,
Ge b'e co 'dh' eòin no 'dh' àlach thu:
Cùm do riar fo reachd do chòt'
'S an gniomh do lòin bi sàr-dhìleas!'

Iasgair:

'Mo thaing is m' eud gu'n robh gu léir dhuit
'Eòin bhig thréin is tàlanta,
Nis gur leur dhomh grunnd do reusoin
'S m' ùidhean féin 'na 'm fàilinneachd,
Tha cainnt do bhéil gun fhàileadh bréige
'S móran céill' ri 'thàrradh bhuait:
Beannachd leat, a ghràidh mo chéile,
Slàint air sgéith 's air ràmhan leat!'

(*DMNC*, pp. 31–32)

The Gull of the Poor Shore

Fisherman:

'Beloved creature, what's the use for you
Of staying about this coastline,
Where you'll not gather anything of beauty
And you a hermit each day.
Would not a more sensible arrangement
Be your living in peace in the bays,
Where there's warm snug lodgings for you
And food from an ungrudging beach?

Tell me, as it baffles me,
What benefit you find in it,
As my eyes see nought but barbarous shore
Dispersing the waves' wrath.
Are you aware that the handline took
from the blue deep what would tempt you,
And the birds of air are all there noisily
Enjoying the gains of their harvesting from it?'

Gull:

'I believe, young boy, your cry rings hollow
And you do not have a knowledge of nature,
Though great's your access to wider wisdom
Your advice is not so profitable.
Though my table is bare of food and ware
In the eyes of decadent higher creatures
I am, still, without want nor care
My mind settled and satisfied.

*What would I desire or want
Given I'm not a slavish glutton?
If I'm content and without agitation,
Do I not have the highest gift?
If my food and shelter are
Not lacking for my mindset and desires
My home's esteem is just as worthy
As though I were a queen's bird.*

*Believe me, lad! It's not your state
Or leisurely luxury that will satisfy you.
Believe me! It's not even the title
To all of Europe above all that.
But what will give you lifelong happiness,
Regardless what bird or species you are:
Keep your wants in line with your coat
And in deeds of food be steadfast!'*

Fisherman:

*'My thanks and pleasure to you entire
Wee bird, wise and wiry,
Now I see the basis of your reasoning
And my self-interests in my failing,
Your mouth's words are without trace of lies
And great wisdom to be had from you:
Farewell, my heart's beloved,
Good health on wings and wave to you.'*

Cainnt mo Mhàthar (1914)

Gach eun san ealtainn sheinneas ceòl
'S e cheileir féin is bòidhche leis;
Bho 'n uiseig choiriollaich 's na neòil,
Gu ruig an dreadhan òg 'sa phreas.
Mar sin tha cinnich agus slòigh,
Mar sin 's ann tha gach pòr air leth:
'S i cainnt am màthar 's cha'n e'n còrr
An ciad thochra 's an còir-bhreith.

'S i cainnt a mhàthar; oighreachd gaoil,
A' chainnt is caoimhe leis gach crè,
'S i cainnt a mhàthar; fonn ro-chaoin
A' chainnt gu'n labhair smaoin a chléibh.
O chànain m' athraichean bho aois!
A chagair laoch nan làith' a thrèig!
Cuim' nach aidichinn gu saor
D' airidheachd air laoim mo spèis?

Cuim' nach aidichinn gu buan
D' airidheachd air uaill is gràdh?
Cuim' nach seasainn thu 's gach uair,
Mar bu dual do shliochd nan sàr?
Carson a leiginn le luchd t'fhuath
Bagairt ort le uaigh no bàs?
Cuim' nach togainn mo ghuth suas
As leth teanga luaidh nam bàrd?

A' Ghàidhlig aosda; cainnt mo rùin,
'S i 'chainnt a dh' ionnsaich mi 'am òig'.
'S i 'thug mo mhàthair dhomh air thùs
'S mi aig a glùin air bheagan treòir.
Is mar nach fhaicinn neach le tnùths

'S a' falt cùbhraidh-se fo 'bhròig;
Mar sin cha chluinntinn mac gun mhùirn
A' deanamh spùirt air cainnt a beòil.

A' chainnt 'san d' fhuair mi oilean m' òig',
'San d' fhuair mi eòlas air na's fhiach,
Gur h-ise dh' fhosgail dhomh air thòs
A dorsan mór' gu tuigse 's ciall.
O 's ise thug dhomh 'n deoch ri 'h-òl!
A blas ri m' bheò gu'm bi 'nam bhial;
A teagasg, achmasan is nòs,
A daonnachd chòrr 's a feara-ghniomh.

'S i 'theagaisg dhomh gach subhailc a mhàin
Tha cumail tàth an clann nan daoin.
'S i 'theagaisg dhomh gu loma làn
Air carantachd, air gràdh is gaol.
Gach uile chomhairle gu m' stàth,
Gach uile ghnàth ann 's an robh saod,
Thug i dhomh an rogha ràdh,
An seanfhacal 's am bàrdachd saor.

Bidh mo chridh' an geall gu bràch
Air cainnt mo mhàthar 's air a ceòl;
Air fuaim nam fonn a sheinn a bàird,
Air pong a clàrsaich 's a piob mhòir,
Fad' 's dh' èireas beann 's a thearnas màm,
Fad's 's chluinnear gàir aig sruth ma'n còir,
Biodh cainnt nan Gàidheal mar a bhà;
A' togail àil gu'n seas a còir.

(*DMNC*, pp. 33–34)[1]

---

1 There's a misprint in *DMNC* in the third verse, which I have corrected above with reference to the original publication in *Guth na Bliadhna*, 11 (1914), pp. 265–67.

My Mother Tongue

Each bird of air that sings its song
Finds its own cry most beautiful;
From the melodious lark in the clouds,
To the young wren in the bush.
Like that are nations and peoples,
Like that is each separate progeny:
It's their mother tongue and not another
That's their tocher and birth right.

It's his mother tongue; love's inheritance,
That's the dearest language to each being,
It's his mother tongue; so tender a melody,
The language that speaks his bosom's thoughts.
O language of my fathers of old!
That the heroes of days gone-by whispered!
Why would I not freely admit
Your worthiness of my abundant fondness?

Why would I not admit forever
Your worthiness of pride and love?
Why would I not stand with you in each hour
As was the way of sons of the heroes?
Why would I permit your haters
To threaten you with grave or death?
Why would I not raise my voice
On behalf of the language the bards sung?

Ancient Gaelic; the language I love,
It's the language I learned in my youth.
It's what my mother gave me first
Whilst I was at her knee with little strength.
And as I wouldn't see a man of bigotry

And her sweet hair under his foot
As such I won't hear a disrespectful lad
Making sport of her mouth's language.

The language in which I received youth's learning
In which I discovered what's valuable,
It was she who opened for me at first
Her great doors to understanding and meaning.
O she gave me drink to drink!
Her taste while I live will be in my mouth;
Her teaching, admonitions and mores,
Her humanity and virtue.

It was she who taught me each virtue alone
That keeps bonds amongst mankind.
It was she who taught me fully
Of charity, of love and affection.
Each counsel that was of use,
Each practice that was of worth,
She gave in choice words,
Proverbs and poetry freely.

My heart will be forever set
On my mother tongue and on her music;
On the sound of tunes sung by her bards,
On the note of her clarsach and great pipe,
Whilst hills rise and valleys fall,
Whilst streams' cries are heard about them,
The Gael's language will be as she was;
Raising her young to defend her rights.

Loch na h-Ob (1915)

Mar dhearrsadh gréine maduinn Màigh
Do sheomar 'carnadh glòir;
Mar sin thig cuimhn' air sealladh àidh
Le ùrachd gràidh gu m' mheòmhair.
Ach thar gach fleadh do'm shùil a bhà
Thar fuinn is sàil is neòil,
Bidh spéis mo chridhe 'laidhe ghnàths
Air àilleachd Loch na h-Ob.

Is ùror blàth sa mhadunn chiùin
A' fosgladh sùl á clò;
Is ùror ribhinn gheal mo rùin
An dreach fo chrùn na h-òig';
Is ùror dorsan dait' an là
'Nan lasair-smàl le bòidhch';
Ach ùroireachd is sin tha 'bharr
Air àilleachd Loch na h-Ob.

Air Loch na h-Ob tha maise naomh
Nach fhaic mi 'n taobh so'n fhòd;
An Loch na h-Ob tha tobar gaoil
Na's cùbhr' na smaoin na h-òigh,
O, 'n sgàthan neamhaidh, soilleir, subhailc!
O, 'n naoidhean suaineach stòld
Ri gràs na Flathas àrd tha suaip
Aig tuar-neul Loch na h-Ob.

Mar shobhrach àluinn 'fàs leath' féin
Air chùl nan sléibhtean mór;
Mar òigh gun smal nach fhaca crè
Bho'n d'fhiosraich beud no bròn;
Mar eun an t-sàil air bhàrr nan stuagh

Gun chùram ruaig no leòn;
Mar sin tha maise, sìth is uaill
Is suaimhneas Loch na h-Ob.

Cha'n ioghnadh sruthan beinn an fhraoich
'Bhi ruith le caoin-ghuth cheòl;
Cha'n ioghnadh bradan mear nan caol
'Bhi leumnaich aotrom òg;
Cha'n ioghnadh leam an fhaoileag bhàn
Le 'gaol a' snàmh gu fòill;
Oir 's sonas uile dhaibh gu bràth
'Bhi tàmh an Loch na h-Ob.

'Se cor na beatha dragh is streup,
'S an cois an streup thig bròn,
Ach cha'n eil galair gun a léigh
Nan robh e lèir do'r n-eòl.
An uair bhios smalan agus gruaim
A' dubhadh duairc mo neòil,
Gheibh m' anam sonas, fois, is cluain
An uaigneas Loch na h-Ob.

A Loch na h-Ob a choisinn m' eud
Mo bheannachd féin ad' chòir!
Do shàmhchair bheannaichte 's do spéis
Bidh 'n dlùths mo chléibh ri m' bheò.
Mo dhùrachd agus m' achain bhuain;
Nach tathaich truaill do chòrs'
Ach bhi 'na d' shealladh maise 's buaidh
Gu'n teirig cuairt nan lò.

(*DMNC*, pp. 40–41)

Loch na h-Ob

Like sun sparkles on a May morning
Filling a room with glory,
Like so, comes a memory of a joyous sight
With love's freshness to my mind.
But above each delight that's been to my eye
Above soil and brine and cloud,
My heart's esteem will ever lie
On the beauty of Loch na h-Ob.

Vivid the bloom in the calm morning
Opening its eye from slumber;
Vivid my heart's white maiden
In form under the crown of youth;
Vivid the coloured doors of day
Alight as embers with beauty;
But there's vividness and more besides
In the beauty of Loch na h-Ob.

On Loch na h-Ob there's a holy beauty
That I won't see this side of the grave;
On Loch na h-Ob there's a well of love
Sweeter than the virgin's thoughts,
O, the heavenly mirror, bright, virtuous!
O, the infant sleepy and sedate
Of high paradise's grace there's a likeness
In the appearance of Loch na h-Ob.

Like the beautiful primrose growing alone
Behind the great hillsides;
Like a faultless maiden not having seen a soul
Who'd tell her of harm or grief;
Like the seabird atop the waves

Without fear of pursuit or woe;
Like so are beauty, love and worth,
The peace of Loch na h-Ob.

No wonder the heather hill's burn
Runs with softly sung tune;
No wonder the narrows' lively salmon
Is leaping lightly, youthfully;
No wonder the fair herring gull
Lovingly swims at ease;
For happiness is theirs for ever
Residing in Loch na h-Ob.

Life's lot is worry and strife
Behind the strife comes grief,
But there's no plague without a cure
If we can know it clearly.
When sorrow and gloom
Darken my hue's frown,
My spirit takes happiness, rest and peace
In the solitude of Loch na h-Ob.

O Loch na h-Ob who earned my praise,
My blessings take to you!
Your blessed silence and your renown
Be treasured in my breast for as long as I live.
My wish and entreaty everlasting;
That no corruption visits your shores
But beauty and victory be in your appearance
Until the course of days has run.

Ròs Aluinn (1917)

O, m' annsachd ort, a Dhealbh na Maise;
'Aiteil chaoin de ghlòir na' Flathas;
'Aisling naomh nan aing'la geala;
'Iomhaigh bheannaichte na h-Oighe!

M' eudail ort, a shùigh mo chéille;
'Aobhneis òig, a Dhòchais éibhinn;
'Ailleagain fo shùil na gréine,
Cha'n eil cruth fo speur cho bòidheach.

'S tusa 'm pong de cheòl nan aingeal
'Thuit an nuas 's a chaochail tannas
'S tusa 'n seud bha 'n uchd na Maidne
An ceud chamhanaich a h-òige.

'S tusa ceud-chruth glòir na Talmhainn,
'S tusa Smaoin nan naoidhean anfhann,
'S tu 'san iar tha nochd ion-dhealbhte
Air brat alla-mhaiseach nan speura.

'S tusa 'n Phòg 'thug Mac na Gile
'Thir nan Òg – a dheòin seach Innis.
'S tusa fòs gu fòil th' air bilean
Oigh mo chridh-sa fo'n éidheann.

'S tu snodha 'n Aoibhneis nach can teanga;
Taibhseal Soillse a chaidh thairis;
Manadh Sòlais a tha maireann;
Tosgaire an gheallaidh nèimhidh.

O, carson do rùgh' cho minig,
'S fàite gàire air do bhilean?
O, carson cho sgaoilt' do chridhe?
Innis dhomh; mur tuigeam féin e.

O, carson am boltradh cùbhraidh
Tha bhàrr d' analach, a mhùirnein?
O, carson an deur 'na chùirnean
Air do shùil an àm dhuit éirigh?

Ma 's e Mac na Spéur do leannan,
'S iomchuidh dhuit do ghnùis is d' anail
Ma 's e 'dheòir an àm 'ur sgaraidh
'Tha thu tasgadh ad' uchd àluinn.

Neo 'n e aon de chlann na sgéithe
'Gheibh do ghaol mar mhil do chléibhe?
O, ma 's e, – carson nach feudadh
Mise féin a bhi de'n àl sin?

M' annsachd ort, a Shùil na Maise,
M' èudail ort, a ghaoil nan leannan
'Shùigh mo chéille, Dia bhi mar riut;
Beannachd leat, a phaidir Màiri.

(*DMNC*, pp. 72–73)

A Beautiful Rose

O, my dearest you, Beauty's Figure;
Tender glimpse of glory in paradise
Sacred dream of the white angels;
Blessed image of the Virgin!

My darling you, my reason's essence
Youthful delight, o cheerful Hope:
Jewel beneath the sun's gaze
There's no form beneath the sky as beautiful.

You're the note of angelic music
That fell from above and faded spectres,
You're the gem that was at Morning's breast
in the first dawn of her youth.

You're the first formed glory of Earth,
You're the Thought of tender infants,
You in the west tonight clearly defined
On the sky's wildly beautiful mantle.

You're the kiss the Son of White gave
To Tìr nan Òg – his desire of all Isles.
You're mild still on the lips of
My heart's maiden under the ivy.

You're the face of Joy no tongue can describe;
Shades of Light that crossed over;
Portent of Solace that is lasting;
Messenger of the heavenly promise.

O, why do you blush so often,
A shy smile on your lips?
O, why is your heart so open?
Tell me; if I don't understand it.

O, why the fragrant scent
That's on your breath, my love?
O, why the tears of dew
On your eyes when you arise?

If the Son of the Sky is your darling
Well-suited to you your aspect and your breath:
If it's his tears at the time of your parting
That you are storing in your beautiful breast.

Or is it one of the children of wings
Who gets your love and bosom's sweetness?
O, if so – why could I not
myself be one of that brood.

My dearest you, Beauty's eye;
My treasure you, lovers' beloved
My reason's essence, God be with you;
A blessing go with you, Mary's rosary.

An Duradan Duslaich (1917)

O, thus' a neòini; thus' a ta cho faoin
Fo chois nan daoi 's nan saoi an diugh 's an dé
Gabh leisgeul bràthar thèid ad' dhàil gu fòil
Ga d' thogail sòluimte gu ruig a leus:
Gu ruig a shùil tha ion is a bhi dall
Am fianuis lampa 'n t-Soluis tha ro chòrr;
'S a spiorad fòs air sgéith, ge breòit' a feart,
Ag iarraidh steach an cridh' an Ioghnaidh Mhóir;
Mar leòmann fhaoin fo ioghnadh is fo cheist,
Le doille-dheil ag iarraidh cridh' a' ghàth,
'S ged thréig a lùths nach toir a dùile suas
Gu 'n tuit i nuas le sgiathan loisgt' air làr.
Oir 's dana 'n gniomh mi dhol gun fhiamh ad' chòir,
Oir tha thu mór; ro-mhór os cionn mo cheud,
Ro-throm a ta; ro-àrd am brìgh 's an ciall –
O, 'dhadmuinn mhiorailtich gabh rium am éis,
Na 'm b' fhiù leat sin ad' mhórachd is ad' aois!
Ad' ùmhlachd naoimh 's ad' iriosalachd làin
Gabh rium-sa truas – tì 's suaraiche 'bha riamh,
Oir 's fianuis thusa 'n sin air Dia nan gràs.
Théid lìnntean seach mar cheò air lear ri oidhch'
Is làmh na gaoithe sior 'g a iùl an céin:
Cha chaochail thusa, 's cha téid thu air dhìth,
Cha 'n eil aig Tìm ort buil no aig an Eug.
Théid righrean daoirs' 'nan culaidh bhaoth car seal,
'S mar shradaig, geal o'n teallach, théid iad aog,
'S am mórachd leamh théid sios mar eas le gleann
A' dol air chall gu beachd an cuan nan aois.
Ach thus bhà 's a chunnaic triall nan linn
Le 'n ceuma sìthe dol o 'n Ear do'n Iar,
'Nad chuimhne mhòr tha dealbh nan lò 's nam fear,
'S ge h-ìosal staid, is tusa 'mhair 's chan 'n iad.

Ge h-ìosal staid, 's tu cioch na beatha fòs;
'S tu céile còir na Màthar móire fial:
'S tu féin le càird do'n aoidh an tràill 's an righ,
'S iad sin gun uidhreachd dhiot, gun mheas, gun fhiach.
Tha daoimean, òr, is seudan òirdhearc, nuadh
An sùilean buairt' mar ghibhtean luachmhor, còrr,
Ach, ann am fàsaich co e 's àirde tairbh',
An daoimean ainmig, no an gaineamh de'n fhòd?
Tha sgil is ìnnleachd cur an ìre 'n sàr
A chur ri àilleachd ealain àrd nan clann,
Ach seall am flùr ud, faic a ghnùis fo bhlàth
'G an cur gu nàire ged 'san dus tha bhonn!
Thig Eòlas pròiseil ann ad' chòir le stràic,
Le gloine 's àsuinn dh' iarraidh dàn do chré, –
An leanabh beag a chaidh a bhreith an raoir
Ag iarraidh 'ghreim a chur ma'n chruinne-ché.
Mar 's diomhain sin, is diomhain sgil nan àl
A thuigsinn fàth an neirt tha 'tàth do nì;
A' chumhachd mhór ud a tha snaim a ghaineamh
Co a dh' airmheas – seach a h-ainm – co i?
Tha Uamhar dall a' riaghladh chlann nan daoin',
A th' air an daoraich le 'n an-saoiltean féin,
Ach, co dha 'n comas, ge h-àrd sgil no buaidh,
Aon ghaineamh suarach 'chur ri Cruthachd Dhé?
O, 'Dhuine bhaoth; a chreutair nan an-miann!
O, c' àit' do ghniomhan, c' àit do thuigse chòrr?
A bheil uil-eòlas dhuit mu nì fo'n ghréin?
A bheil ort féin dhuit eòlas beag an tòs?
Tha grian nan tràth a ghnàth ri falach-fead
Ma'n cuairt a' ché, ach tha clann bheag fo leòn;
Clann bheag a ta le'n sùil an sàil an cos,
Ach léigh an cor cha leugh iad sin 'san fhòid.
O, thugam taing dhuit, thusa Choibhneis Mhòir
An éirig pòir nach aidich còir no luach:

An éirig bheò le 'n iasad-dheò 'nan cléibh
A shaoileas breun an dus gu'm féum iad uaigh.
Ged dheanadh doill air tàir le 'n casan dorch',
'S am bodhaig choirbt' air chrith os cionn a sgùird,
Cha tig air gruaim ri àl neo-bhuan gun chéill,
'S ann bheir e déirce dhaibh le barrachd rùin.
A Ghaineamh, is bràithrean sinn; mi féin is tù:
'S sinn gniomh is cùram an aon Ughdair àird.
O, gabham sùileachan o d' ùmhlachd féin,
Air chor 's gu'n éirich mi am measg do bhlàth.

(*DMNC*, pp. 65–66)

The Speck of Dust

O, you, nothing; you who are so trifling
Underfoot the wicked and wise today and yesterday,
Excuse your brother gently coming to you
Lifting you solemnly to reach his gaze:
To reach his eye that is as good as blind
In the presence of the lamp of super abounding Light;
And his spirit yet aflight, though his strength be broken,
Wanting to enter the heart of the Great Unknown:
As the futile moth in wonder and curiosity,
With blind perseverance seeking the heart of the ray
And though its powers fail it will not give up its goal
Until it falls with burnt wings to the floor.
For bolder is the deed my approaching you without
      trepidation
For you are great – too great above my ken
Too weighty; too high in meaning and reason –
O miraculous atom accept me in my need,
If you esteem that in your greatness and your age!
In your sacred lowliness and complete humility
Have pity on me – as worthless as a being has been,
For you are a witness there to the God of grace.
Ages pass like mist on the sea at night
And the wind's hand ever steering it abroad:
You do not change, you do not go amiss,
Time does not impact you, or death.
Oppressive kings become laughing stocks a while,
Like a spark, white from the hearth, they die,
And their polished majesty goes down like the waterfall in
      the glen
Getting lost to thought in the sea of age.
But you were there and saw the ages' journey

With their forceful steps going from East to West,
In your great memory are the forms of days and men,
Though low's your state, it's you, not they, who persist.
Though low's your state you are life's breast yet;
You're the kindly spouse of the great generous Mother:
Yourself friendly with guest, slave and king,
And they without interest in you, regard or value.
Diamond, gold and noble jewels, vivid
In muddied eyes are like valuable, hearty gifts,
But, in the desert who has more worth
The rare diamond, or the grain from a sod?
Skill and intellect claim to add their best
To the beauty of their offspring's high art,
But consider that flower, see its countenance in bloom
Putting them to shame, though its base is in the dust!
Proud Knowledge comes into your presence with a clatter,
With glass and apparatus seeking your core's ken –
The little babe that was born last night
Wanting to grasp the universe.
As futile as that is, futile is the skill of that lot
In understanding the cause of the strength that binds you;
The great power that ties its grain
Who can compute – rather than name – it?
Blind Pride rules the sons of men,
Who're drunk on their own conceits,
But, who is able, though high in skill and powers
To add one lowly grain to God's Creation?
O, foolish Man; creature of wanton desire!
O, where are your deeds, where is your great knowledge?
Do you truly understand anything under the sun?
Do you have even a little understanding of the beginning?
The season's sun is ever hiding and seeking
About its worldly spouse, but small children are wounded;

Small children whose sight lies under the foot's tread,
But healing their state, they won't read that in the grave's sods.
I give thanks to you, Great Kindness,
In reparation for a race who do not admit right or worth:
In reparation for those living with borrowed breath in their chests
Who think the earth corrupt till they need a tomb.
Though the blind may despise it with their darkening feet,
And their corrupted body shaking above its lap,
Displeasure will not come on him for a clueless transient generation,
Rather he'll give them alms with greater love.
Speck of sand, we're brothers; me and you:
We are deeds and charges of the same great Author.
O, I will take my lesson from your very humility,
So that I will arise amidst your bloom.

Slighe nan Seann Seun (1930)

Saoibhir sìth nan sian an nochd air Tìr-an-Aigh,
Is ciùine ciùil nam fiath ag iadhadh Innse Gràidh,
Is èasgaidh gach sgiath air fianlach dian an Dàin,
Is slighe nan seann seun a' siaradh siar gun tàmh.

Saoibhir com nan cruach le cuimhne làithean aosd',
Sona gnùis nan cuan am bruadair uair a dh'aom;
Soillseach gach uair an aigne suaimhneach ghaoth –
O! làithean mo luaidh, 'ur n-uaill, 'ur n-uails', ur gaoil!

O! làithean geala gràidh le 'gnàthan geala còir,
O! aimsireanan àigh le 'r gàire, gean is ceòl –
O! shaoghail nan gràs, nan gathan aithne 's eòil,
C'uime thréig 's nach d' fhàg ach àilte àin ur glòir'?

An ioghnadh deòin is dùil bhi dol a null 'nar déidh,
Ri ionndruinn nan rùn a lion 'ur sgùird le spéis?
An ioghnadh ceòl nan dùl bhi seinn air cliù 'ur réim,
Is fabhra crom gach sùl' bhi tàis fo dhùbhradh léug?

A làithean sin a thriall le ial-luchd àis mo shluaigh,
C'uime thàrr 'ur miann gach dias a b'fhiachmhor buaidh?
An ioghnadh an iarmailt shiar bhi nochd fo shnuadh,
'S 'ur n-àrosan an cian bhi laist' le lias bith-bhuan?

An ioghnadh lom gach làir bhi 'luaidh air làn 'ur sgeòil?
An ioghnadh cnuic is ràdh a chomha-thràth 'nam beoil?
An ioghnadh cruit nan dàn bhi bìth fo sgàil' a neòil –
Is ealaidh-ghuth nam bàrd gun seun, gun sàire seòil?

Cha neonach cill mo shluaigh an cois nan cuan bhi balbh,
Chan ioghnadh uchd nan tuam bhi 'n tòic le luach na dh'fhalbh,
O, shaoghail, is truagh nach tìll aon uair a shearg,
'S nach tàrr mo dheòin, ge buan, aon fhios á suain nam marbh!

(*DMNC*, p. 96)

The Way of the Old Charms

Rich is the elements' peace tonight on the Land of Joy
Quiet is the calm's melody around the Isle of Love,
Nimble is each wing on the eager warriors of Fate
And the way of the old charms, stumbles West without rest.

Rich the mounds' body with memories of olden days,
Happy the sea's aspect in a dream of a time that's waned;
Shining each hour beneath the wind's peaceful spirit –
O! my beloved days, your pride, your nobility, your love!

O! the bright days of love with your kind pure ways,
O! times of joy, with your laughter, wit and music –
O! world of grace, rays of knowledge and wisdom,
Why did you depart leaving only the noble light of your
    glory?

Is it a surprise that will and hope follow on behind you,
Missing the warmth that filled your folds with affection?
Is it a surprise the world's music sings the esteem of your
    rule,
And every bent lash wet beneath a darkening jewel?

Those days that left with the plentiful wisdom of my people,
Why did your desire pull each sheaf most precious and
    excellent?
Is it a surprise the western heavens tonight are beautiful,
Your far-off palaces lit with an eternal light?

Is it a wonder that each floor's bareness recounts the
    fullness of your tale?
Is it a wonder the knolls have the dusk's sayings in their
    mouths?

*Is it a wonder the harp of songs is silent underneath its
    clouds –*
*The fluent voice of the poets without charms, or excellent
    technique?*

Not strange that my people's kirkyard by the sea is silent
*No wonder the tombs' breasts are swollen with the worth
    that's gone,*
*O, world, it's a pity that not one hour that's faded will
    return,*
*And that my will, though enduring, won't draw one word
    from the dead's slumber!*

www.ingramcontent.com/pod-product-compliance
Ingram Content Group UK Ltd.
Pitfield, Milton Keynes, MK11 3LW, UK
UKHW020117170126
467079UK00007B/38